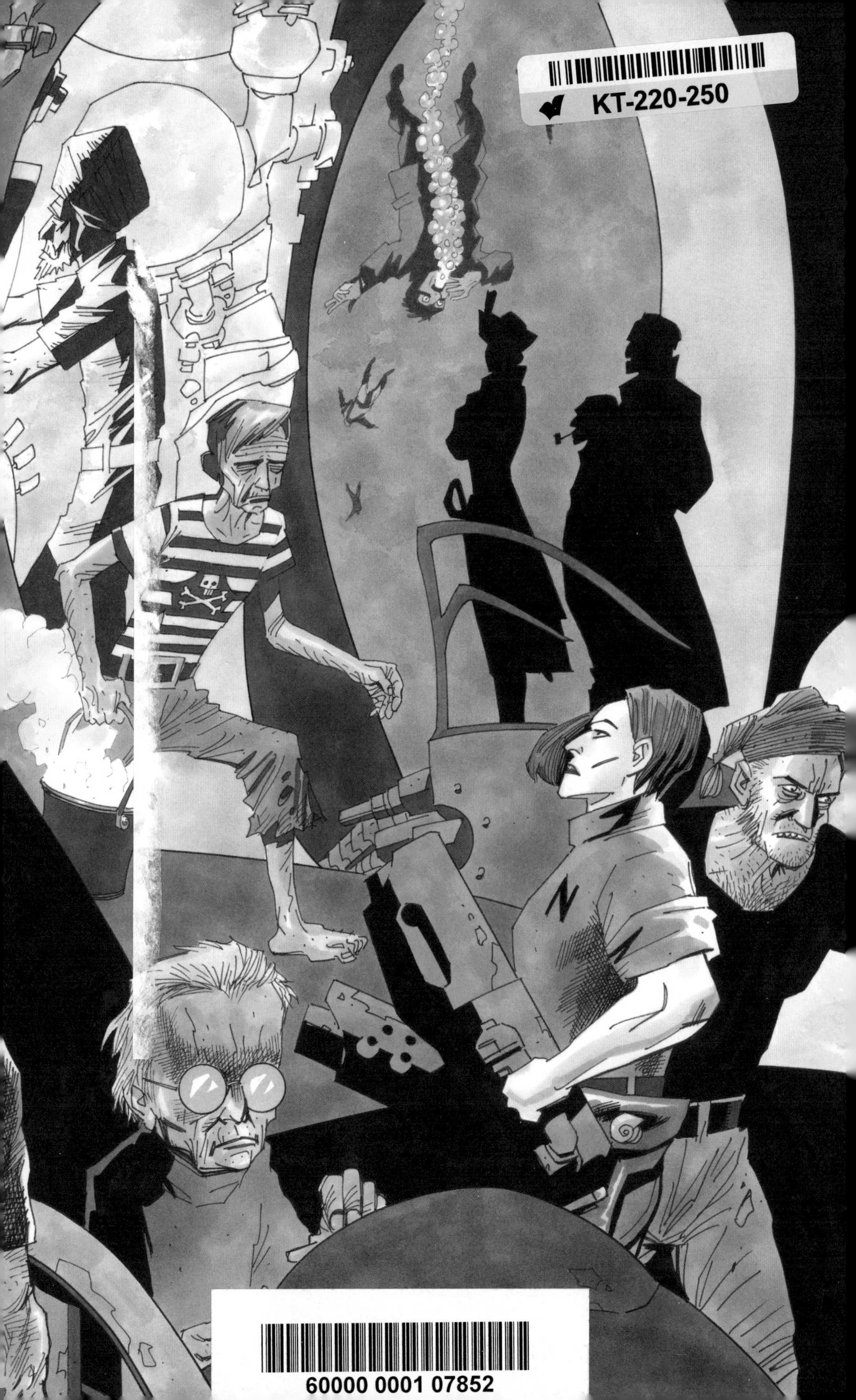

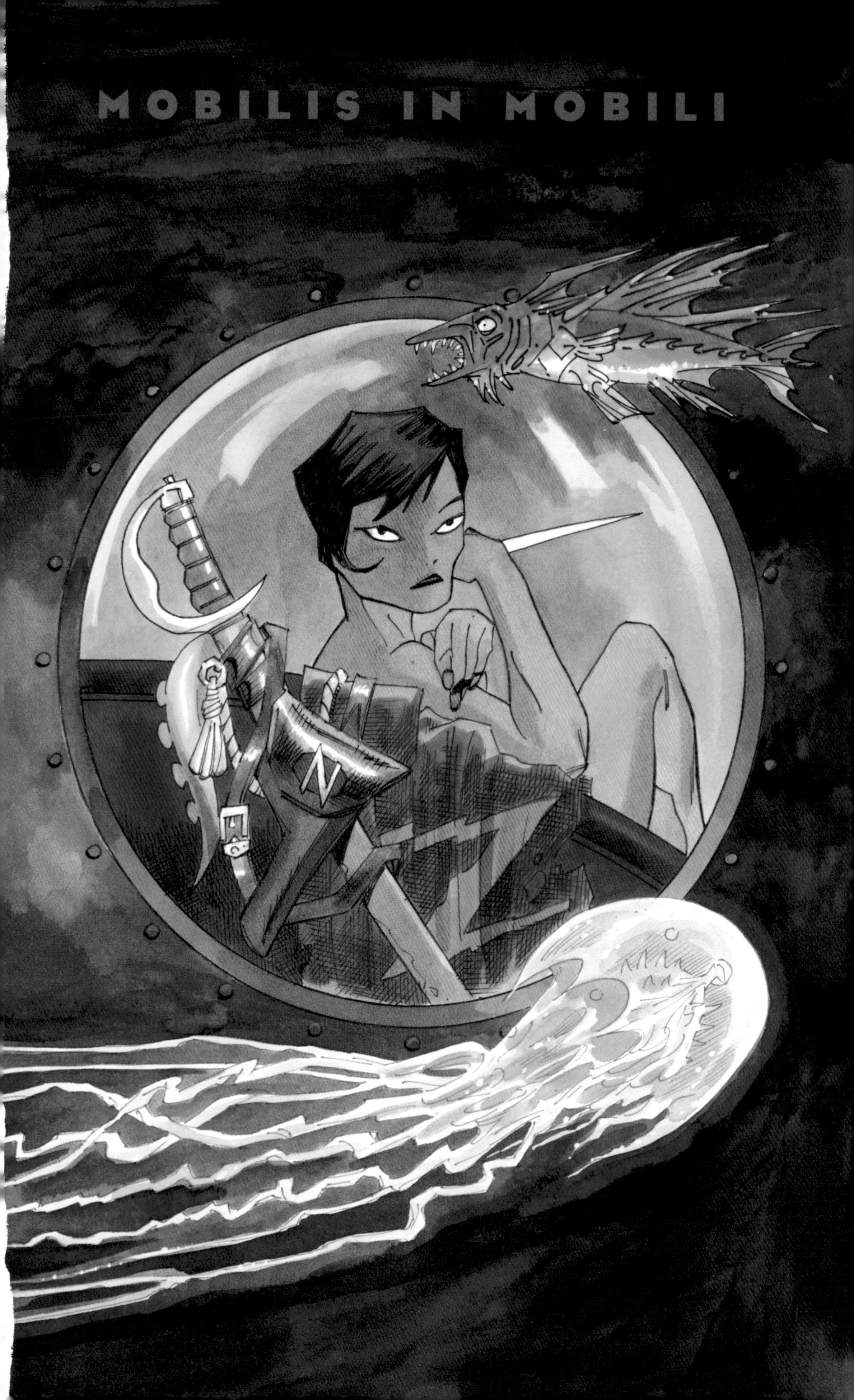
MOBILIS IN MOBILI

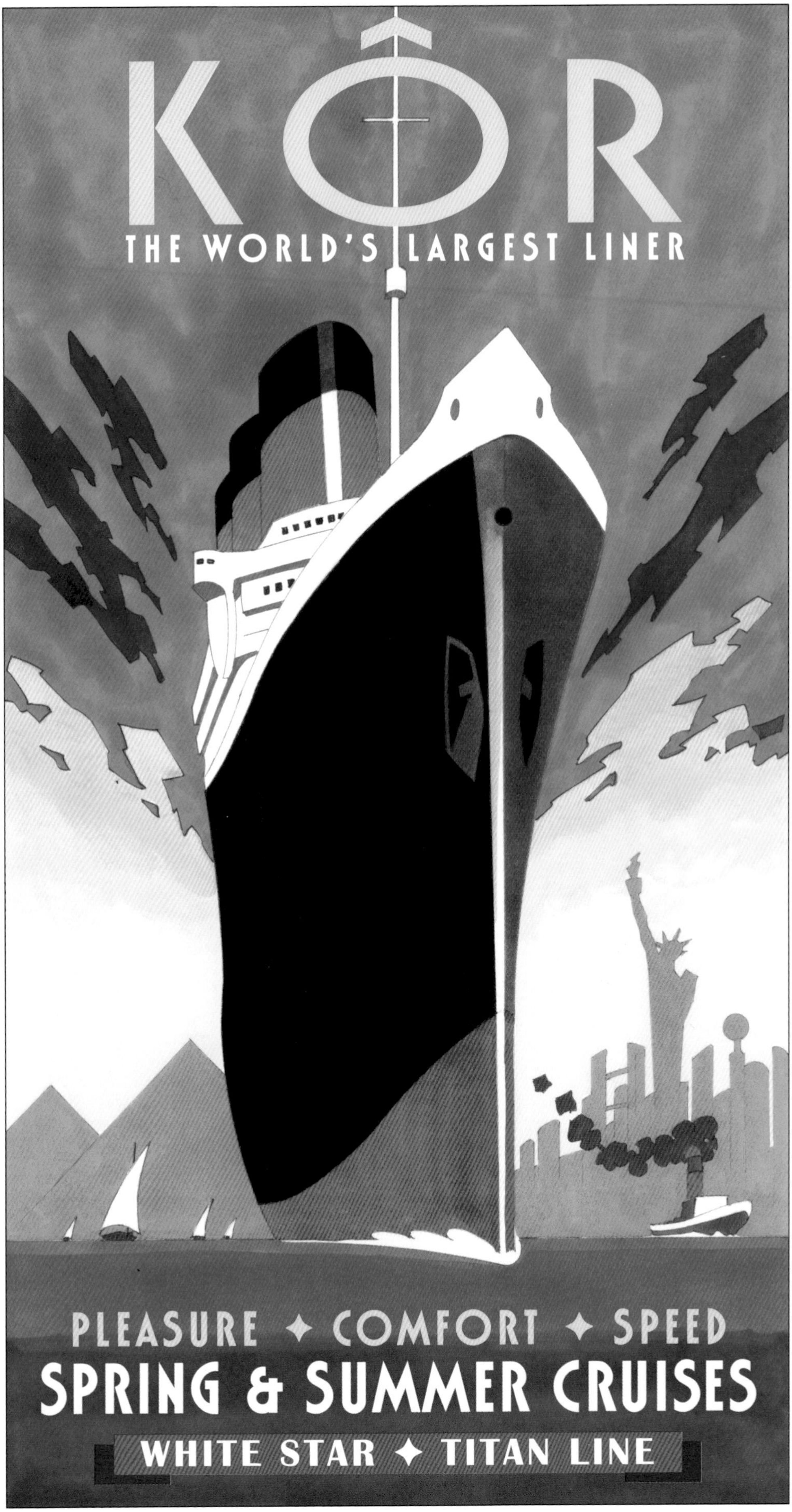
KÔR
THE WORLD'S LARGEST LINER
PLEASURE ✦ COMFORT ✦ SPEED
SPRING & SUMMER CRUISES
WHITE STAR ✦ TITAN LINE

# — NOTICE —

## THE FOLLOWING CREW WILL REPORT TO AFT DECK FOR DISCIPLINE. by ORDER N

| NAME | CHARGE |
| --- | --- |
| ALAN MOORE<br>Hemp Master and Manatee keeper | Shanty writing most fearful and creating reefer knots for gain. |
| KEVIN O'NEILL<br>Jack of all Trades and Master of Rum | Tattooing comic cuts on passenger's booty. |
| TODD KLEIN<br>Marooner | Graffito and lewd design. |
| BEN DIMAGMALIW<br>Master of false Colours | Dazzle painting Mr. Mates' rude ape. |
| SCURVY LOWER DECK and BRIGANDS | |
| TONY BENNETT and JOSH PALMANO | Knockabout behaviour and suspected publishers. |
| CHRIS STAROS and BRETT WARNOCK | Found with Top Shelf material and suspected publishers. |
| SEAMAN STAINES | Possession of an offensive name. |

MAY YOUR GOD 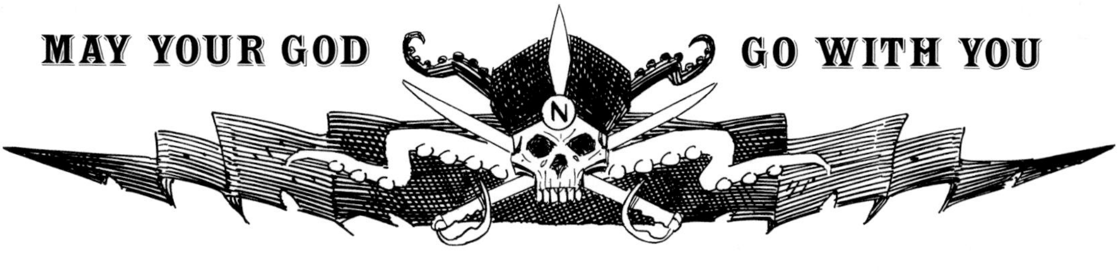 GO WITH YOU

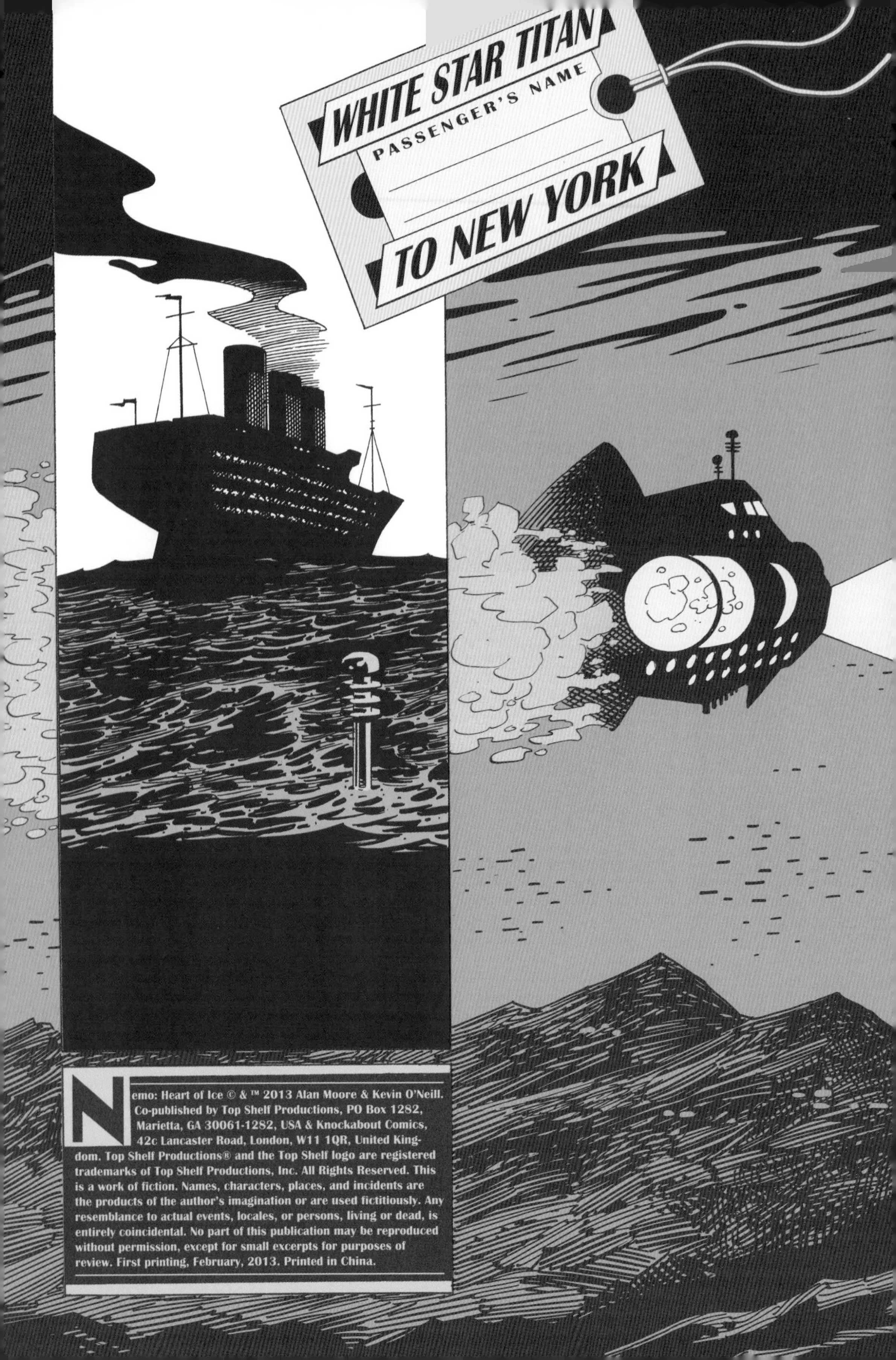
WHITE STAR TITAN
PASSENGER'S NAME
TO NEW YORK

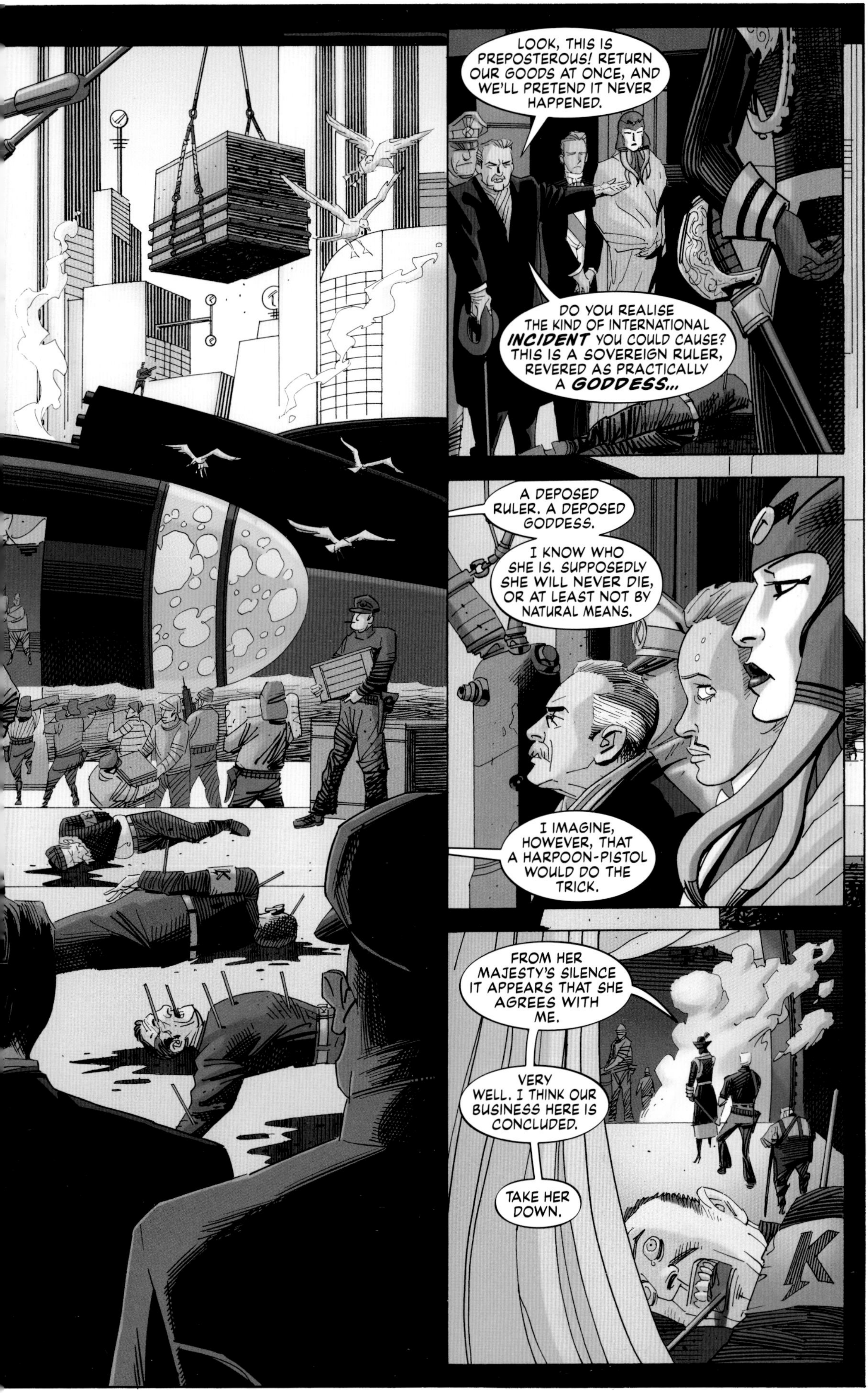
LOOK, THIS IS PREPOSTEROUS! RETURN OUR GOODS AT ONCE, AND WE'LL PRETEND IT NEVER HAPPENED.
DO YOU REALISE THE KIND OF INTERNATIONAL *INCIDENT* YOU COULD CAUSE? THIS IS A SOVEREIGN RULER, REVERED AS PRACTICALLY A *GODDESS...*
A DEPOSED RULER. A DEPOSED GODDESS.
I KNOW WHO SHE IS. SUPPOSEDLY SHE WILL NEVER DIE, OR AT LEAST NOT BY NATURAL MEANS.
I IMAGINE, HOWEVER, THAT A HARPOON-PISTOL WOULD DO THE TRICK.
FROM HER MAJESTY'S SILENCE IT APPEARS THAT SHE AGREES WITH ME.
VERY WELL. I THINK OUR BUSINESS HERE IS CONCLUDED.
TAKE HER DOWN.

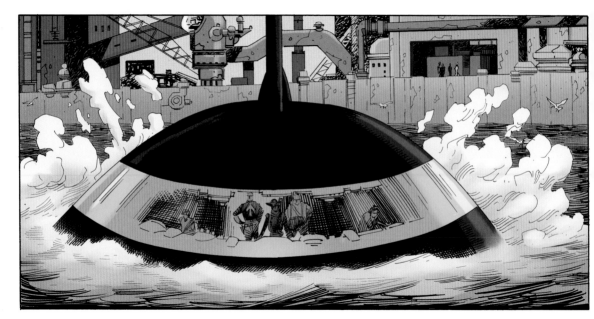

UNBELIEVABLE! REST ASSURED, YOUR MAJESTY, MY EMPLOYEES WILL TRACK THEM DOWN.

Y-YOU SEE, MY QUEEN? MR. KANE CORRECTS EVERYTHING. HE...

YOU DID NOTHING.

B-BUT...

BUT THERE WERE SO MANY. I--I COULD NOT RISK THEM HARMING YOU.

PLEASE, MY QUEEN, DO NOT BE ANGRY. MR. KANE WILL...

...make...

GREAT GOD...

IT DID NOTHING.

GET RID OF IT.

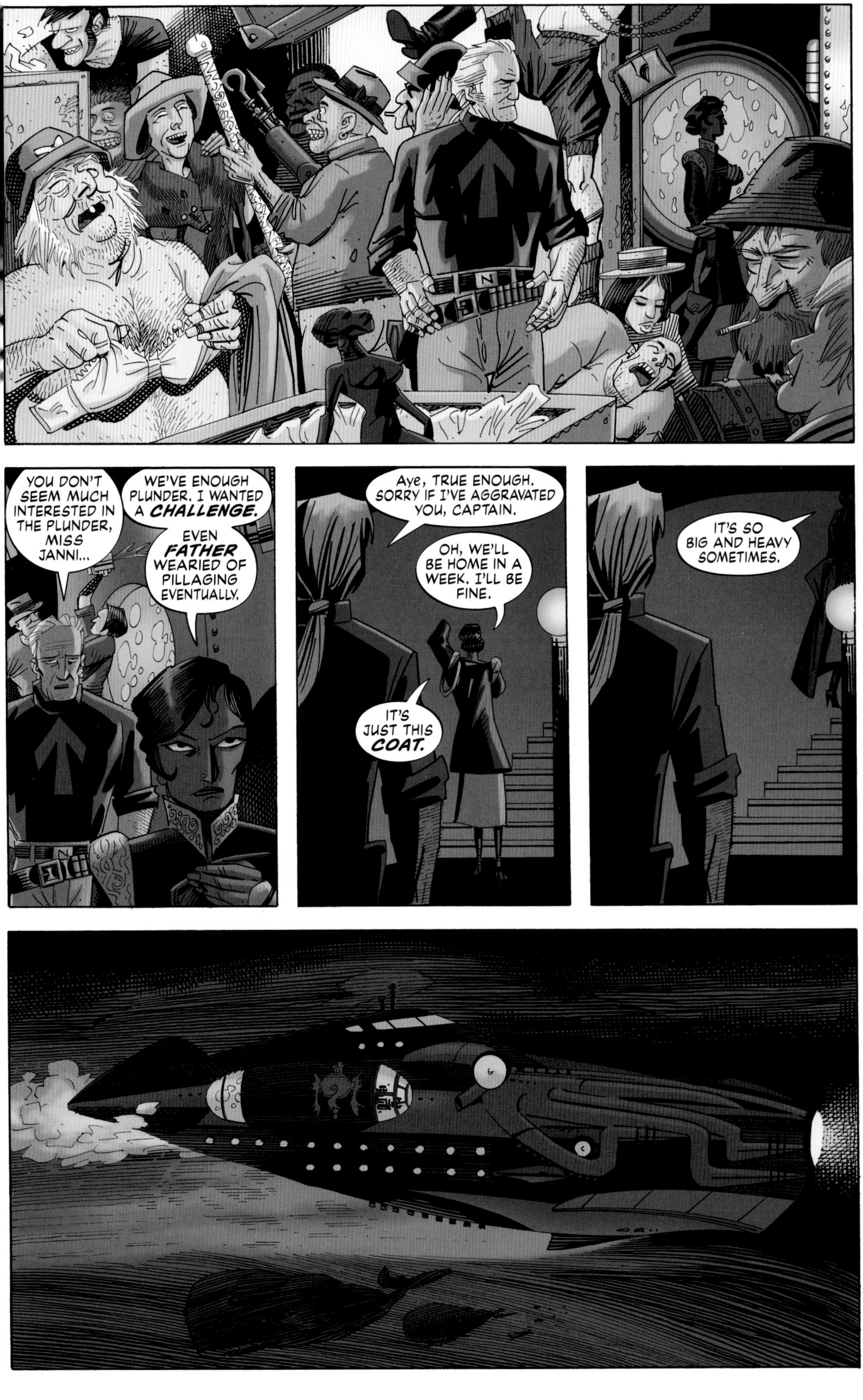
YOU DON'T SEEM MUCH INTERESTED IN THE PLUNDER, MISS JANNI...
WE'VE ENOUGH PLUNDER. I WANTED A CHALLENGE.
EVEN FATHER WEARIED OF PILLAGING EVENTUALLY.
Aye, TRUE ENOUGH. SORRY IF I'VE AGGRAVATED YOU, CAPTAIN.
OH, WE'LL BE HOME IN A WEEK. I'LL BE FINE.
IT'S JUST THIS COAT.
IT'S SO BIG AND HEAVY SOMETIMES.

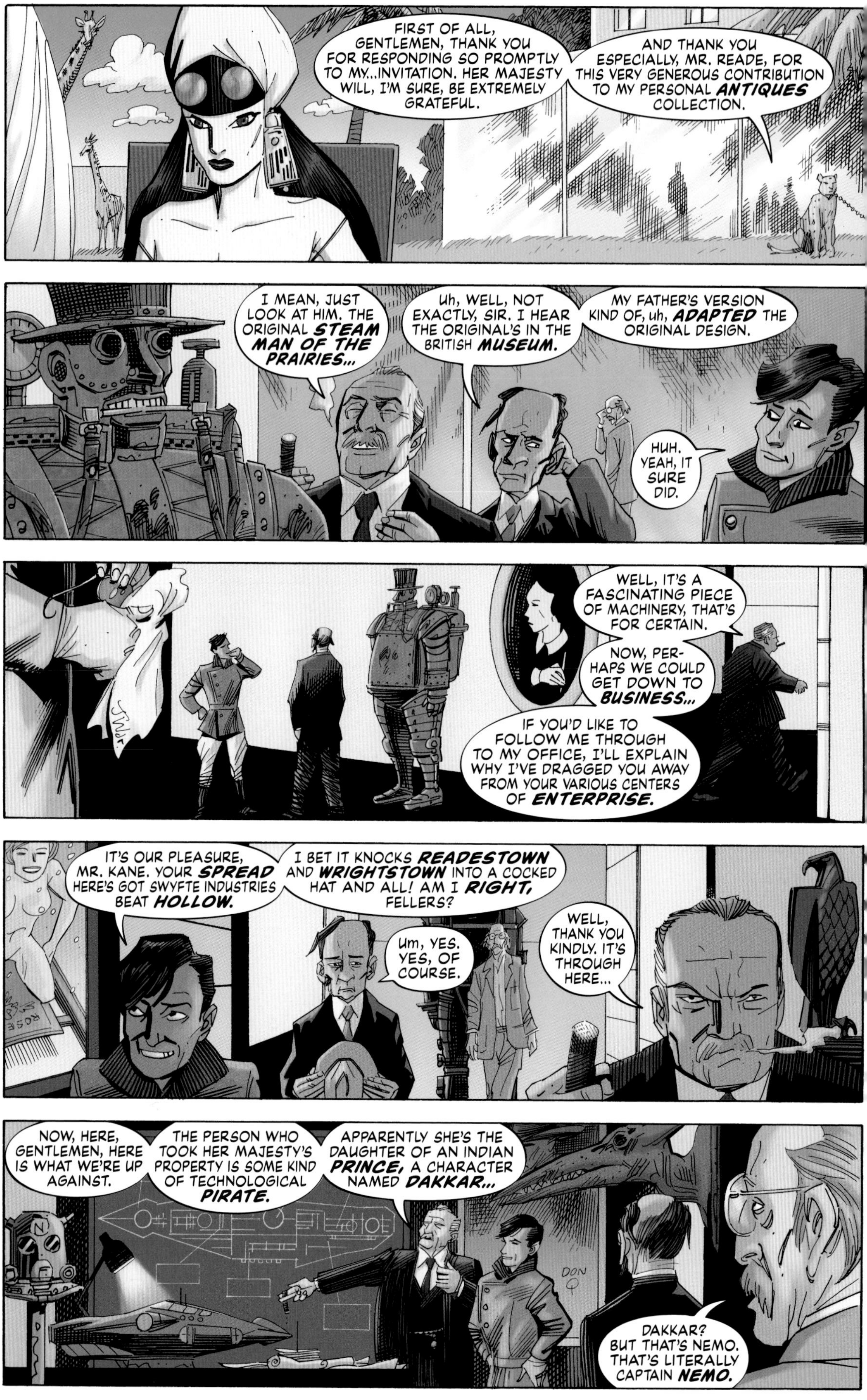
FIRST OF ALL, GENTLEMEN, THANK YOU FOR RESPONDING SO PROMPTLY TO MY...INVITATION. HER MAJESTY WILL, I'M SURE, BE EXTREMELY GRATEFUL.
AND THANK YOU ESPECIALLY, MR. READE, FOR THIS VERY GENEROUS CONTRIBUTION TO MY PERSONAL ANTIQUES COLLECTION.
I MEAN, JUST LOOK AT HIM. THE ORIGINAL STEAM MAN OF THE PRAIRIES...
Uh, WELL, NOT EXACTLY, SIR. I HEAR THE ORIGINAL'S IN THE BRITISH MUSEUM.
MY FATHER'S VERSION KIND OF, uh, ADAPTED THE ORIGINAL DESIGN.
HUH. YEAH, IT SURE DID.
WELL, IT'S A FASCINATING PIECE OF MACHINERY, THAT'S FOR CERTAIN.
NOW, PER-HAPS WE COULD GET DOWN TO BUSINESS...
IF YOU'D LIKE TO FOLLOW ME THROUGH TO MY OFFICE, I'LL EXPLAIN WHY I'VE DRAGGED YOU AWAY FROM YOUR VARIOUS CENTERS OF ENTERPRISE.
IT'S OUR PLEASURE, MR. KANE. YOUR SPREAD HERE'S GOT SWYFTE INDUSTRIES BEAT HOLLOW.
I BET IT KNOCKS READESTOWN AND WRIGHTSTOWN INTO A COCKED HAT AND ALL! AM I RIGHT, FELLERS?
Um, YES. YES, OF COURSE.
WELL, THANK YOU KINDLY. IT'S THROUGH HERE...
NOW, HERE, GENTLEMEN, HERE IS WHAT WE'RE UP AGAINST.
THE PERSON WHO TOOK HER MAJESTY'S PROPERTY IS SOME KIND OF TECHNOLOGICAL PIRATE.
APPARENTLY SHE'S THE DAUGHTER OF AN INDIAN PRINCE, A CHARACTER NAMED DAKKAR...
DAKKAR? BUT THAT'S NEMO. THAT'S LITERALLY CAPTAIN NEMO.

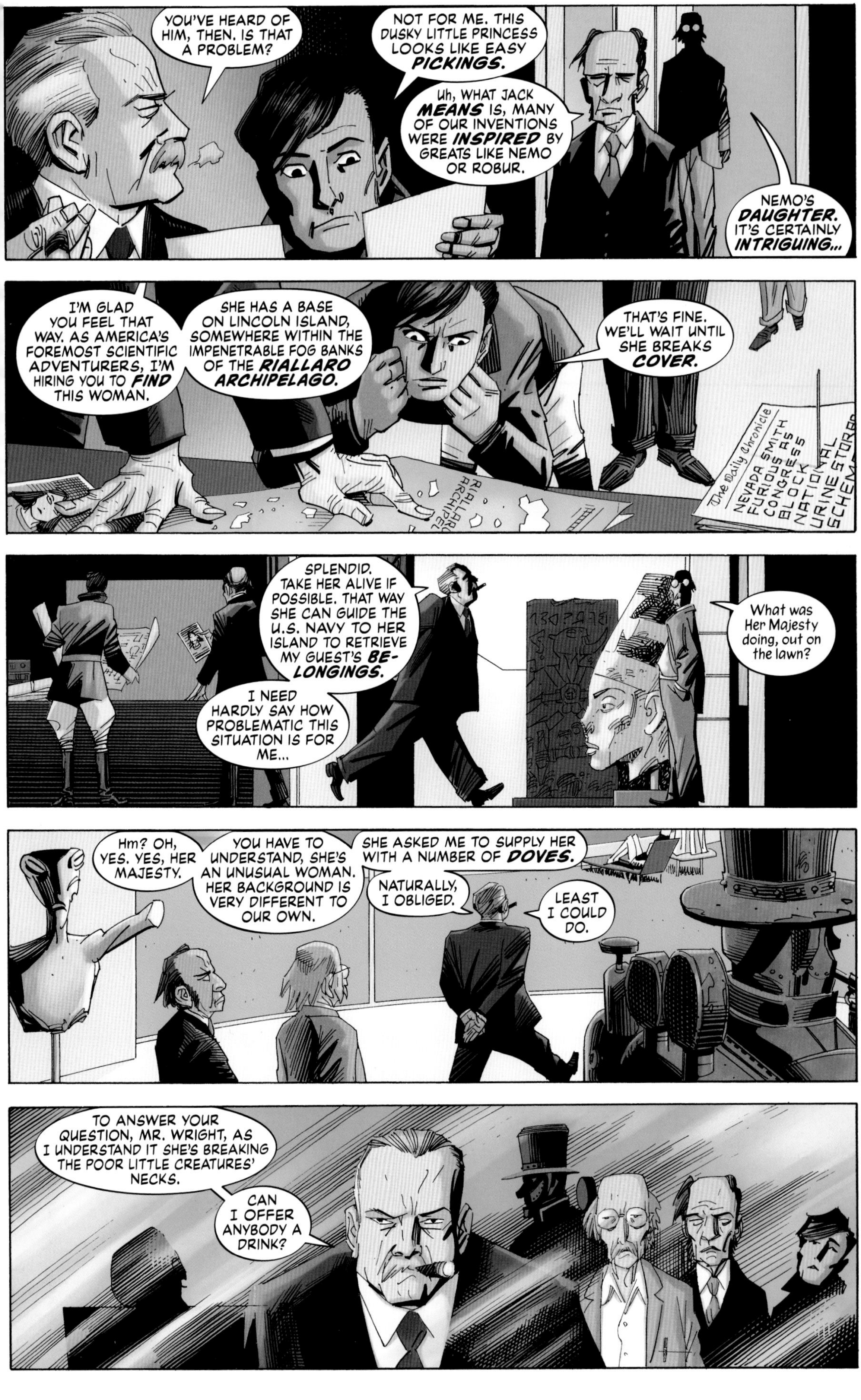
YOU'VE HEARD OF HIM, THEN. IS THAT A PROBLEM?
NOT FOR ME. THIS DUSKY LITTLE PRINCESS LOOKS LIKE EASY PICKINGS.
Uh, WHAT JACK MEANS IS, MANY OF OUR INVENTIONS WERE INSPIRED BY GREATS LIKE NEMO OR ROBUR.
NEMO'S DAUGHTER. IT'S CERTAINLY INTRIGUING...
I'M GLAD YOU FEEL THAT WAY. AS AMERICA'S FOREMOST SCIENTIFIC ADVENTURERS, I'M HIRING YOU TO FIND THIS WOMAN.
SHE HAS A BASE ON LINCOLN ISLAND, SOMEWHERE WITHIN THE IMPENETRABLE FOG BANKS OF THE RIALLARO ARCHIPELAGO.
THAT'S FINE. WE'LL WAIT UNTIL SHE BREAKS COVER.
The Daily Chronicle
NEVADA SMITH FURIOUS AS CONGRESS BLOCK NATIONAL URINE STORE SCHEM
SPLENDID. TAKE HER ALIVE IF POSSIBLE. THAT WAY SHE CAN GUIDE THE U.S. NAVY TO HER ISLAND TO RETRIEVE MY GUEST'S BE-LONGINGS.
I NEED HARDLY SAY HOW PROBLEMATIC THIS SITUATION IS FOR ME...
What was Her Majesty doing, out on the lawn?
Hm? OH, YES. YES, HER MAJESTY.
YOU HAVE TO UNDERSTAND, SHE'S AN UNUSUAL WOMAN. HER BACKGROUND IS VERY DIFFERENT TO OUR OWN.
SHE ASKED ME TO SUPPLY HER WITH A NUMBER OF DOVES.
NATURALLY, I OBLIGED.
LEAST I COULD DO.
TO ANSWER YOUR QUESTION, MR. WRIGHT, AS I UNDERSTAND IT SHE'S BREAKING THE POOR LITTLE CREATURES' NECKS.
CAN I OFFER ANYBODY A DRINK?

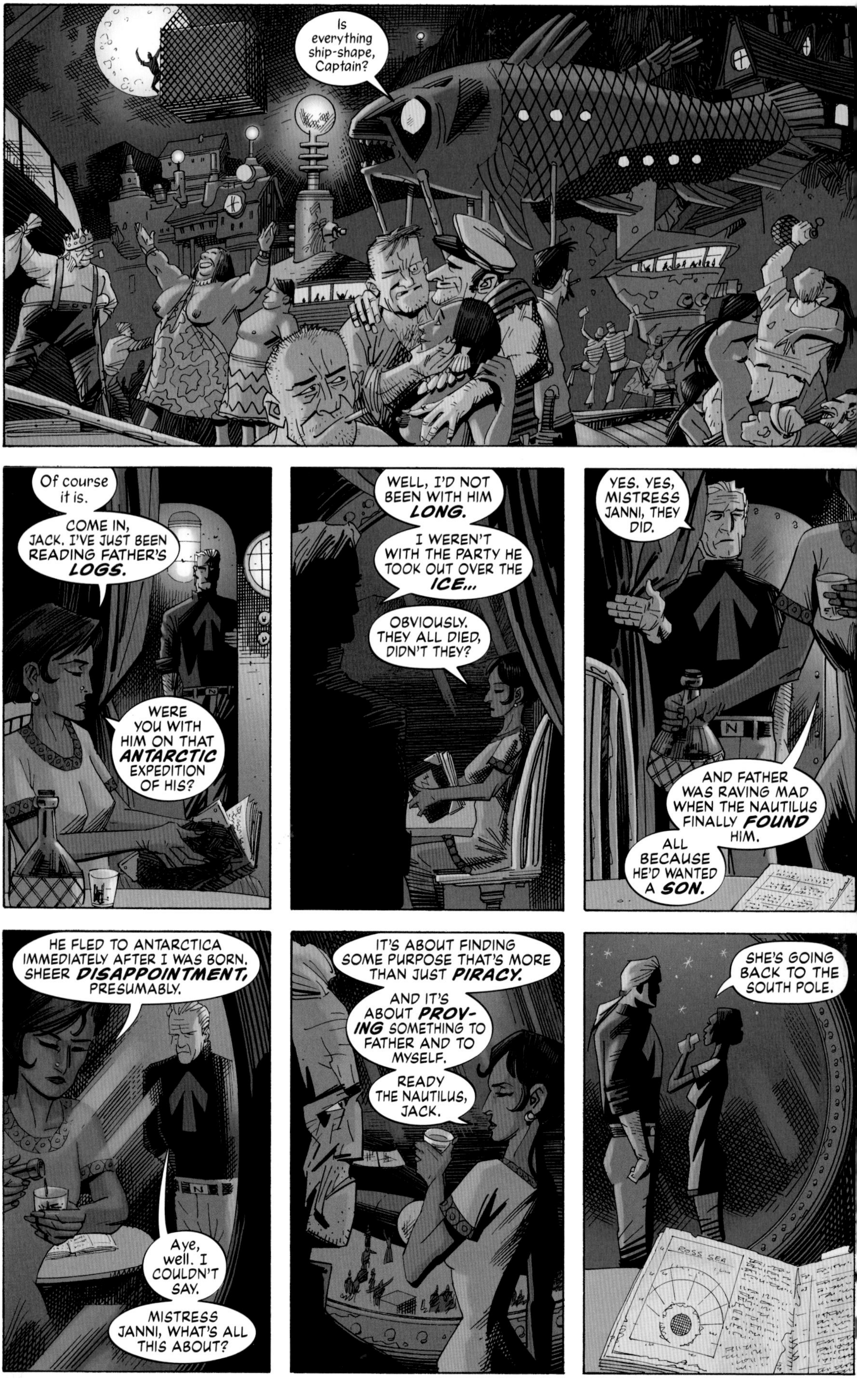
Is everything ship-shape, Captain?
Of course it is.
COME IN, JACK. I'VE JUST BEEN READING FATHER'S LOGS.
WERE YOU WITH HIM ON THAT ANTARCTIC EXPEDITION OF HIS?
WELL, I'D NOT BEEN WITH HIM LONG.
I WEREN'T WITH THE PARTY HE TOOK OUT OVER THE ICE...
OBVIOUSLY. THEY ALL DIED, DIDN'T THEY?
YES. YES, MISTRESS JANNI, THEY DID.
AND FATHER WAS RAVING MAD WHEN THE NAUTILUS FINALLY FOUND HIM.
ALL BECAUSE HE'D WANTED A SON.
HE FLED TO ANTARCTICA IMMEDIATELY AFTER I WAS BORN. SHEER DISAPPOINTMENT, PRESUMABLY.
Aye, well. I COULDN'T SAY.
MISTRESS JANNI, WHAT'S ALL THIS ABOUT?
IT'S ABOUT FINDING SOME PURPOSE THAT'S MORE THAN JUST PIRACY.
AND IT'S ABOUT PROVING SOMETHING TO FATHER AND TO MYSELF.
READY THE NAUTILUS, JACK.
SHE'S GOING BACK TO THE SOUTH POLE.
ROSS SEA

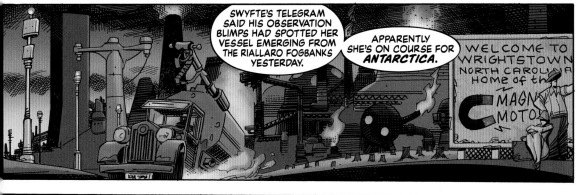

SWYFTE'S TELEGRAM SAID HIS OBSERVATION BLIMPS HAD SPOTTED HER VESSEL EMERGING FROM THE RIALLARO FOGBANKS YESTERDAY.

APPARENTLY SHE'S ON COURSE FOR *ANTARCTICA.*

WELCOME TO WRIGHTSTOWN NORTH CAROLINA HOME of the MAGN MOTO

Why? WHAT'S ANTARCTICA GOT THAT'S WORTH LOOTING?

INCIDENTALLY, JACK, I'M VERY IMPRESSED BY WHAT YOU'VE DONE WITH *WRIGHTS-TOWN.* LOOKS LIKE AN EFFICIENT *SETUP.*

THANK YOU. IT'S MOSTLY BASED ON CARL ROTWANG'S BERLIN METROPOLIS, OBVIOUSLY.

TELL ME, HOW DO YOU LIKE *SWYFTE?*

Humh. TO BE HONEST, I DON'T.

THAT LITTLE PRICK IS LANDING ALL THE CONTRACTS *WE* USED TO GET, JACK, AND HIS ELECTRIC *RIFLE'S* A PIECE OF *JUNK...*

Oh, I don't know. WISH I'D THOUGHT OF IT.

HOPEFULLY, WE'LL BEAT HIM TO *ANTARCTICA.*

I SURE HOPE SO. THE WAY HE'S SUCKING UP TO *KANE,* HE...

HOLY COW! THIS IS YOUR *VEHICLE* HANGAR?

THAT'S RIGHT. BETWEEN HERE AND *READESTOWN,* WE SHOULD HAVE THE WHERE-WITHAL TO OUTSHINE SWYFTE.

WHETHER WE CAN OUTRUN *NEMO'S* TECHNOLOGY IS ANOTHER *MATTER.*

GRANTED, NOVELTIES LIKE THIS ARE PRETTY *NIFTY,* BUT WE DON'T KNOW THE NAUTILUS'S CURRENT *CAPA-BILITIES.*

EVEN NEARLY THIRTY *YEARS* AGO IT WAS CRIPPLING MARTIAN *TRIPODS.*

IF NEMO'S DAUGHTER EMBARKED YESTERDAY, SHE'LL ALREADY HAVE TRAVELLED BEYOND SOUTH AMERICAN WATERS.

SHE COULD BE ANYWHERE.

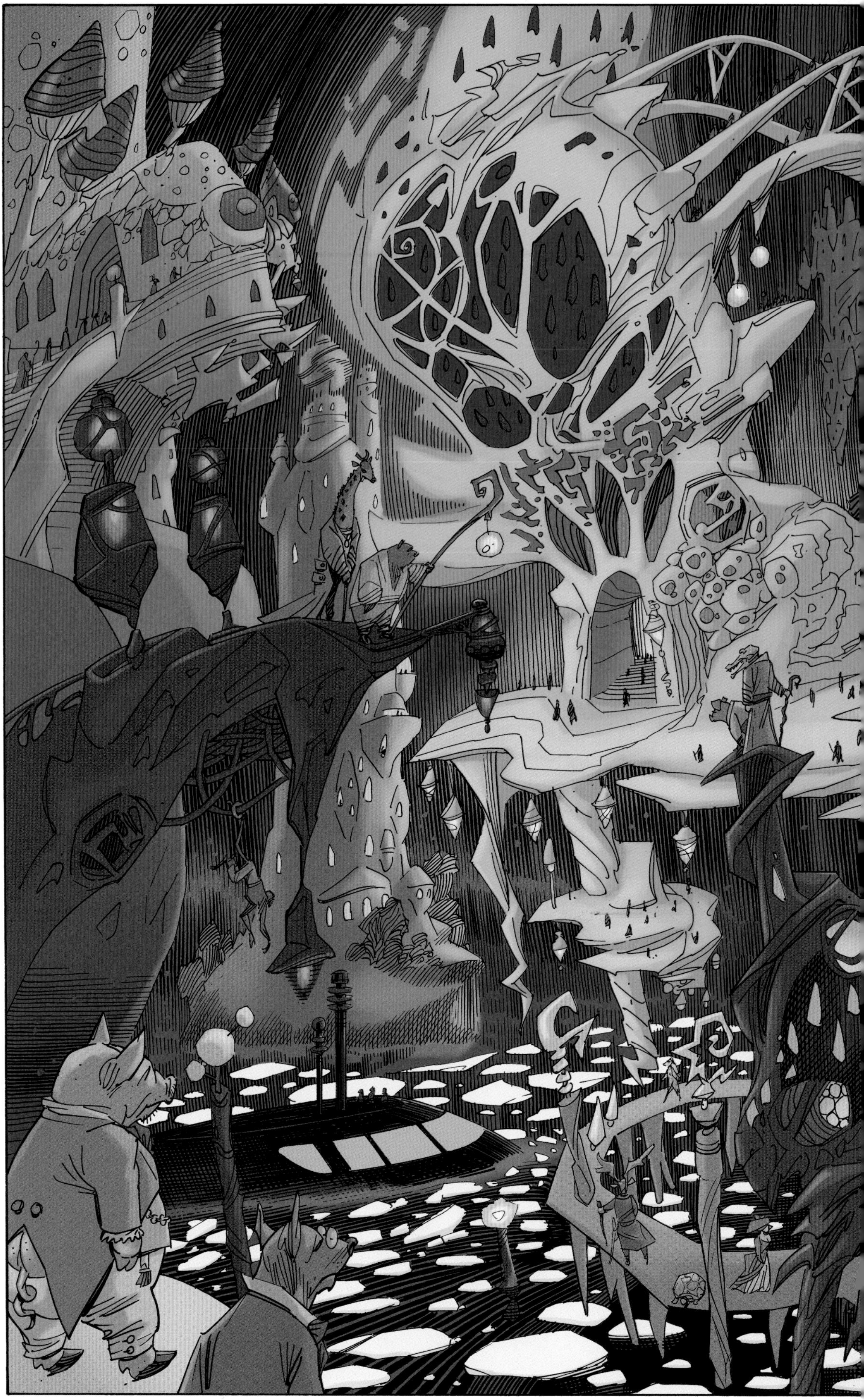

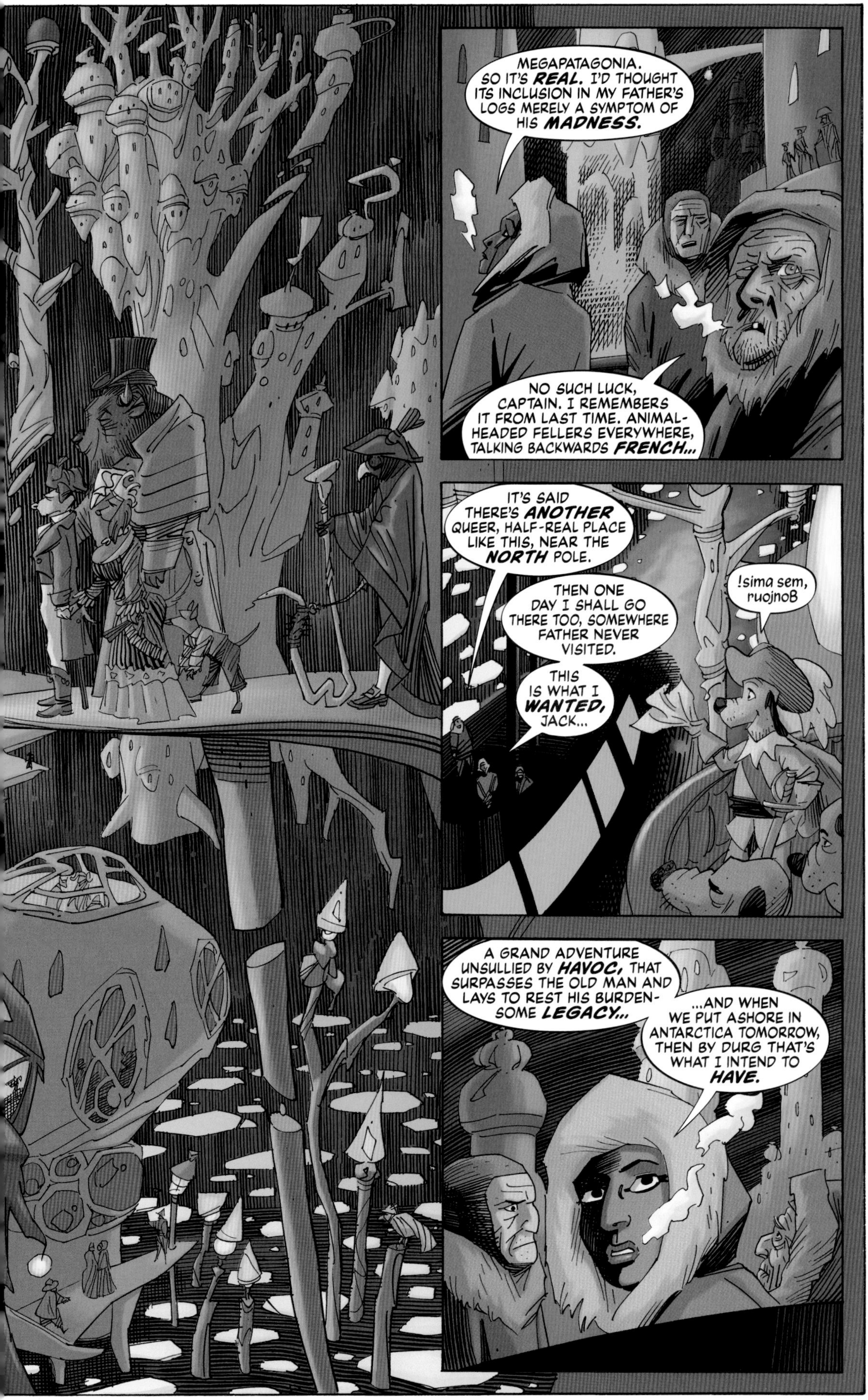
MEGAPATAGONIA. SO IT'S REAL. I'D THOUGHT ITS INCLUSION IN MY FATHER'S LOGS MERELY A SYMPTOM OF HIS MADNESS.
NO SUCH LUCK, CAPTAIN. I REMEMBERS IT FROM LAST TIME. ANIMAL-HEADED FELLERS EVERYWHERE, TALKING BACKWARDS FRENCH...
IT'S SAID THERE'S ANOTHER QUEER, HALF-REAL PLACE LIKE THIS, NEAR THE NORTH POLE.
THEN ONE DAY I SHALL GO THERE TOO, SOMEWHERE FATHER NEVER VISITED.
THIS IS WHAT I WANTED, JACK...
!sima sem, ruojnoB
A GRAND ADVENTURE UNSULLIED BY HAVOC, THAT SURPASSES THE OLD MAN AND LAYS TO REST HIS BURDEN-SOME LEGACY...
...AND WHEN WE PUT ASHORE IN ANTARCTICA TOMORROW, THEN BY DURG THAT'S WHAT I INTEND TO HAVE.

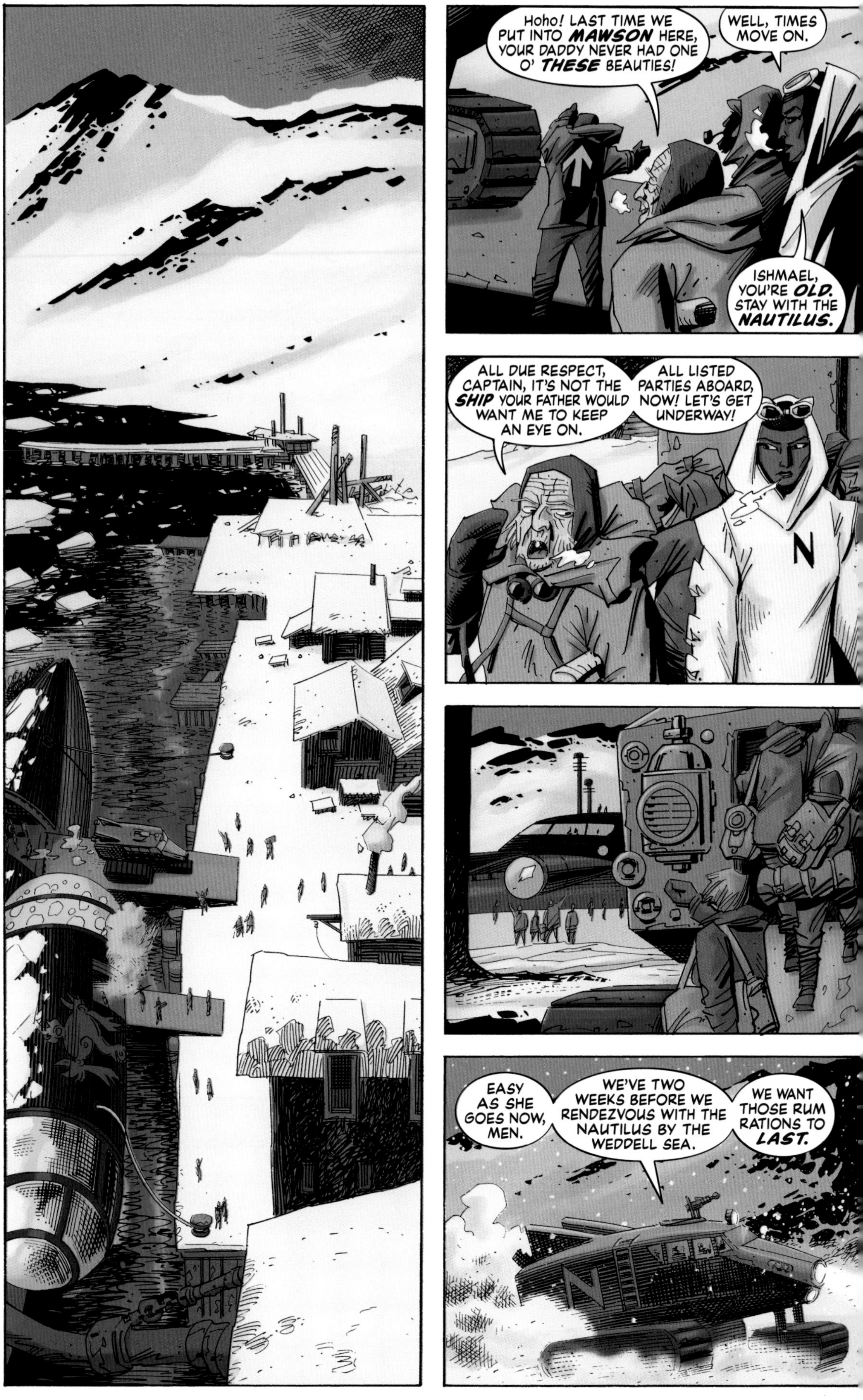
Hoho! LAST TIME WE PUT INTO MAWSON HERE, YOUR DADDY NEVER HAD ONE O' THESE BEAUTIES!
WELL, TIMES MOVE ON.
ISHMAEL, YOU'RE OLD. STAY WITH THE NAUTILUS.
ALL DUE RESPECT, CAPTAIN, IT'S NOT THE SHIP YOUR FATHER WOULD WANT ME TO KEEP AN EYE ON.
ALL LISTED PARTIES ABOARD, NOW! LET'S GET UNDERWAY!
EASY AS SHE GOES NOW, MEN.
WE'VE TWO WEEKS BEFORE WE RENDEZVOUS WITH THE NAUTILUS BY THE WEDDELL SEA.
WE WANT THOSE RUM RATIONS TO LAST.

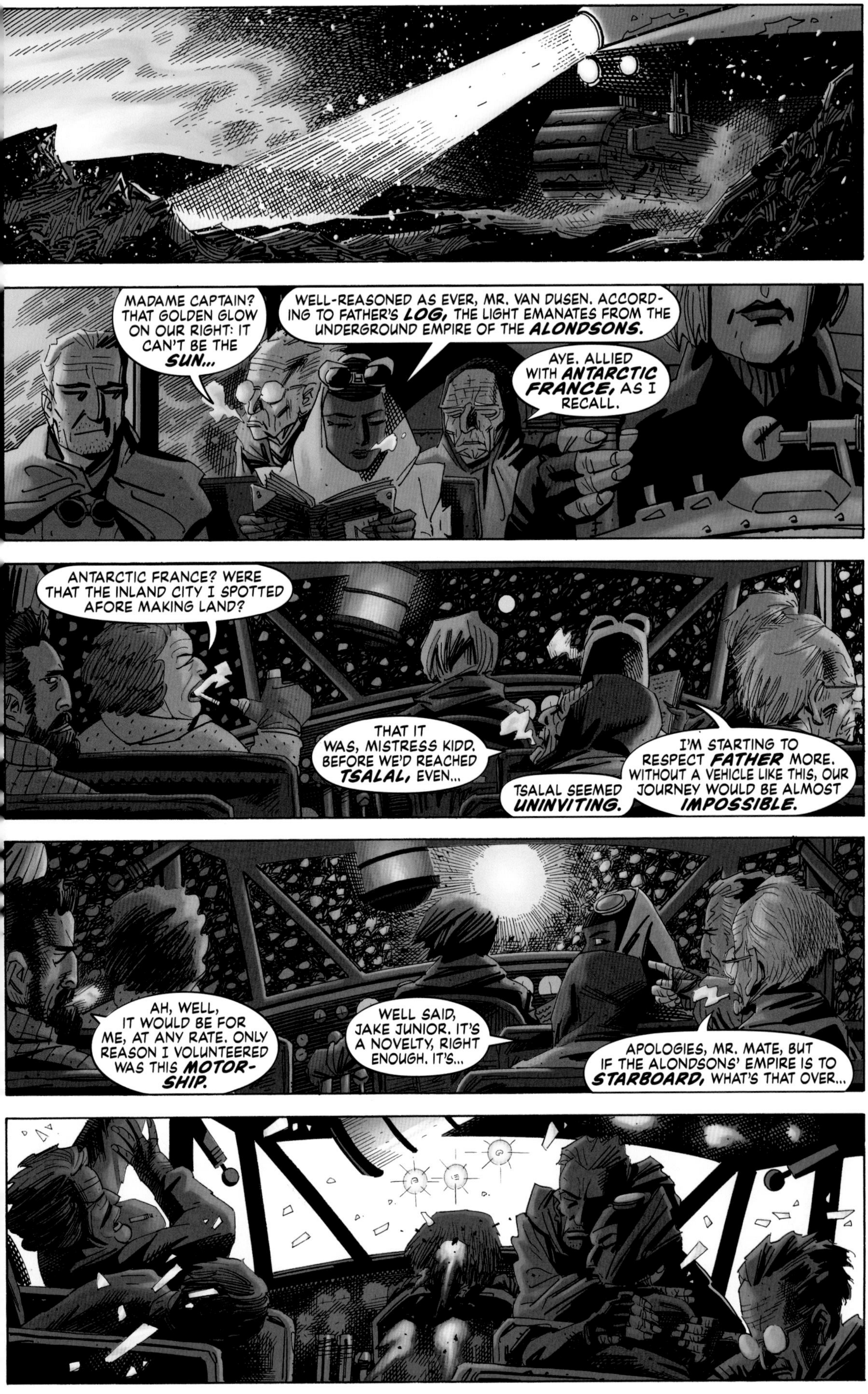
MADAME CAPTAIN? THAT GOLDEN GLOW ON OUR RIGHT: IT CAN'T BE THE SUN...
WELL-REASONED AS EVER, MR. VAN DUSEN. ACCORDING TO FATHER'S LOG, THE LIGHT EMANATES FROM THE UNDERGROUND EMPIRE OF THE ALONDSONS.
AYE. ALLIED WITH ANTARCTIC FRANCE, AS I RECALL.
ANTARCTIC FRANCE? WERE THAT THE INLAND CITY I SPOTTED AFORE MAKING LAND?
THAT IT WAS, MISTRESS KIDD. BEFORE WE'D REACHED TSALAL, EVEN...
TSALAL SEEMED UNINVITING.
I'M STARTING TO RESPECT FATHER MORE. WITHOUT A VEHICLE LIKE THIS, OUR JOURNEY WOULD BE ALMOST IMPOSSIBLE.
AH, WELL, IT WOULD BE FOR ME, AT ANY RATE. ONLY REASON I VOLUNTEERED WAS THIS MOTOR-SHIP.
WELL SAID, JAKE JUNIOR. IT'S A NOVELTY, RIGHT ENOUGH. IT'S...
APOLOGIES, MR. MATE, BUT IF THE ALONDSONS' EMPIRE IS TO STARBOARD, WHAT'S THAT OVER...

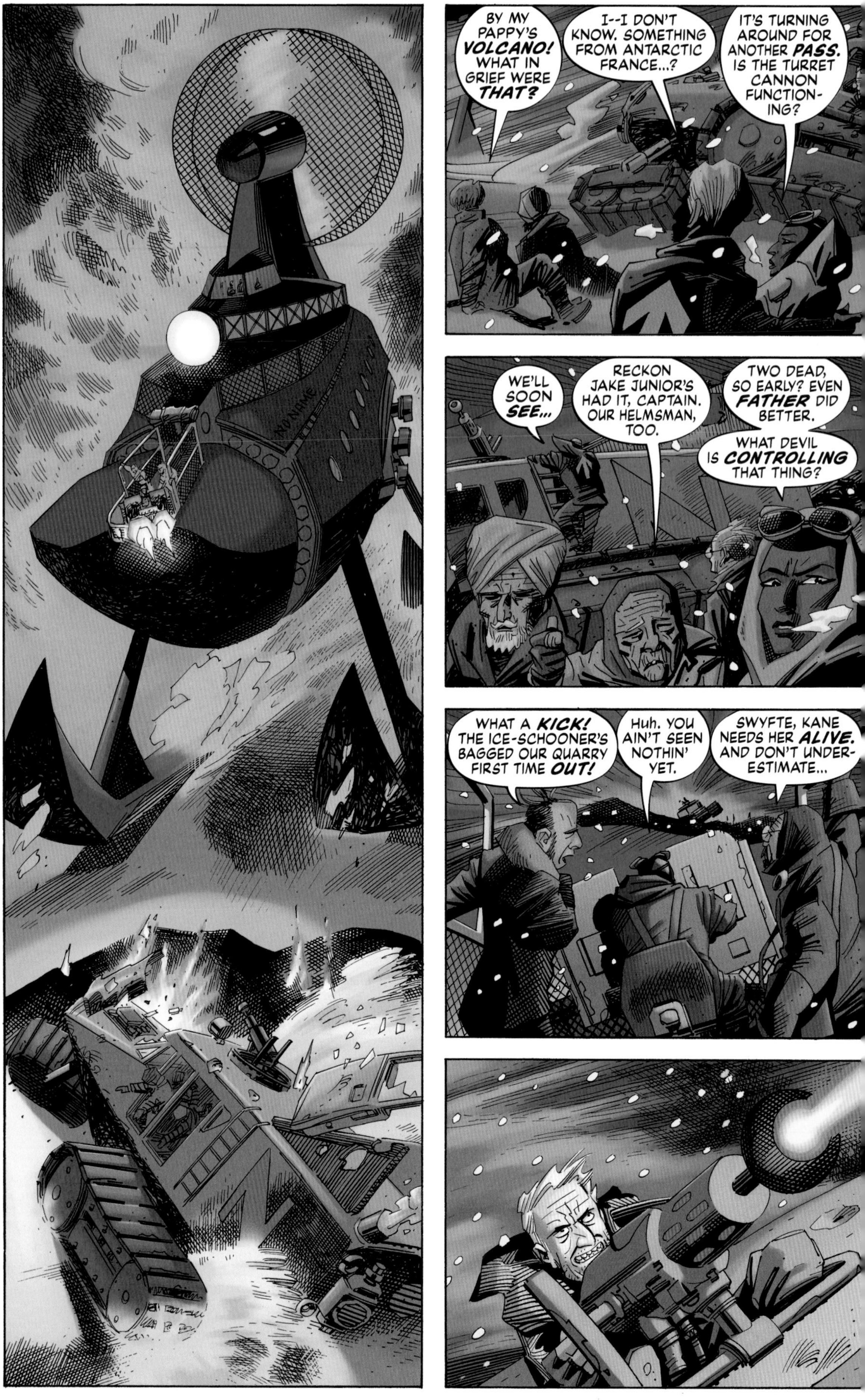

BY MY PAPPY'S VOLCANO! WHAT IN GRIEF WERE THAT?
I--I DON'T KNOW. SOMETHING FROM ANTARCTIC FRANCE...?
IT'S TURNING AROUND FOR ANOTHER PASS. IS THE TURRET CANNON FUNCTION-ING?
WE'LL SOON SEE...
RECKON JAKE JUNIOR'S HAD IT, CAPTAIN. OUR HELMSMAN, TOO.
TWO DEAD, SO EARLY? EVEN FATHER DID BETTER.
WHAT DEVIL IS CONTROLLING THAT THING?
WHAT A KICK! THE ICE-SCHOONER'S BAGGED OUR QUARRY FIRST TIME OUT!
Huh. YOU AIN'T SEEN NOTHIN' YET.
SWYFTE, KANE NEEDS HER ALIVE. AND DON'T UNDER-ESTIMATE...

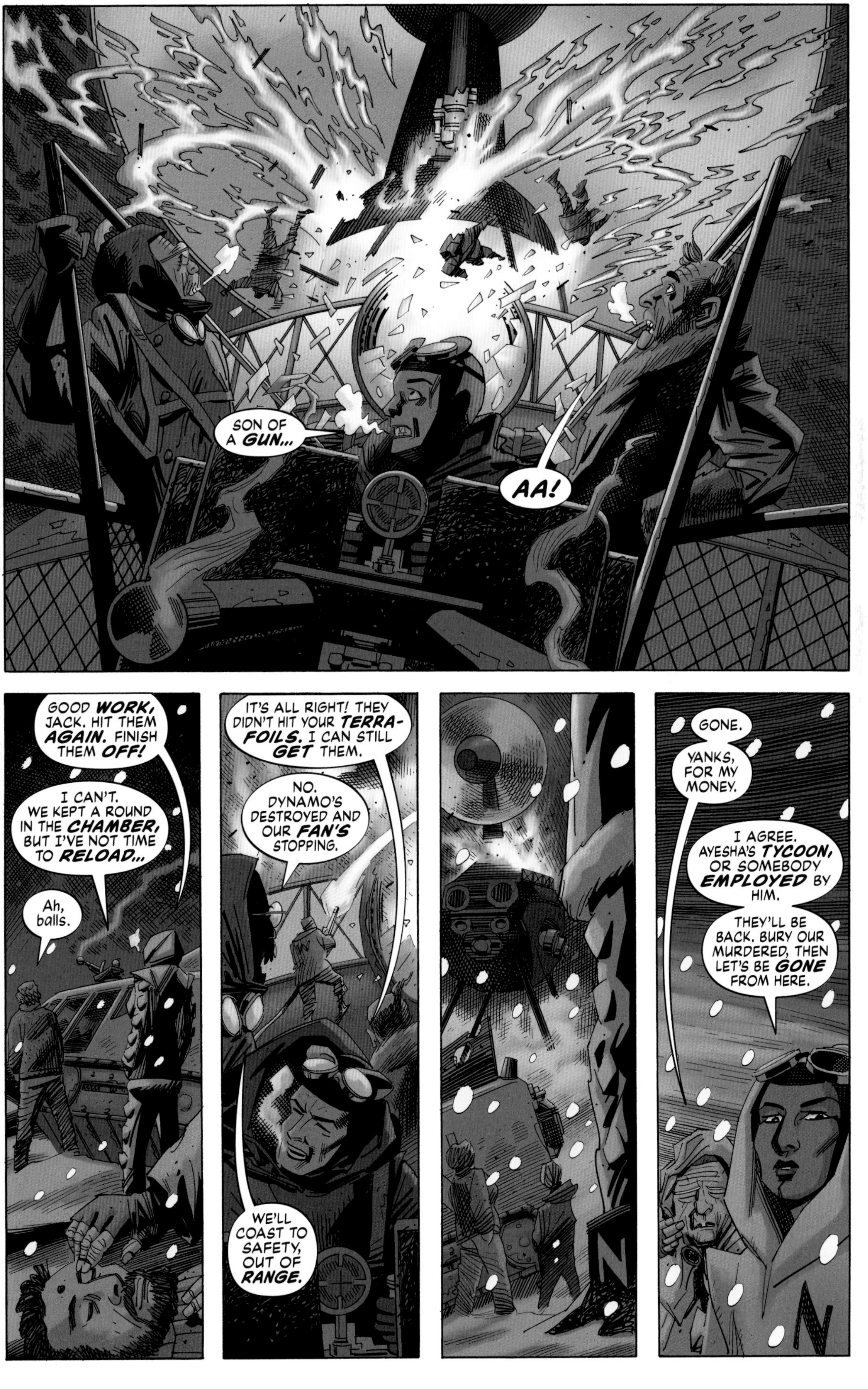
SON OF A GUN...
AA!
GOOD WORK, JACK. HIT THEM AGAIN. FINISH THEM OFF!
I CAN'T. WE KEPT A ROUND IN THE CHAMBER, BUT I'VE NOT TIME TO RELOAD...
Ah, balls.
IT'S ALL RIGHT! THEY DIDN'T HIT YOUR TERRA-FOILS. I CAN STILL GET THEM.
NO. DYNAMO'S DESTROYED AND OUR FAN'S STOPPING.
WE'LL COAST TO SAFETY, OUT OF RANGE.
GONE.
YANKS, FOR MY MONEY.
I AGREE. AYESHA'S TYCOON, OR SOMEBODY EMPLOYED BY HIM.
THEY'LL BE BACK. BURY OUR MURDERED, THEN LET'S BE GONE FROM HERE.

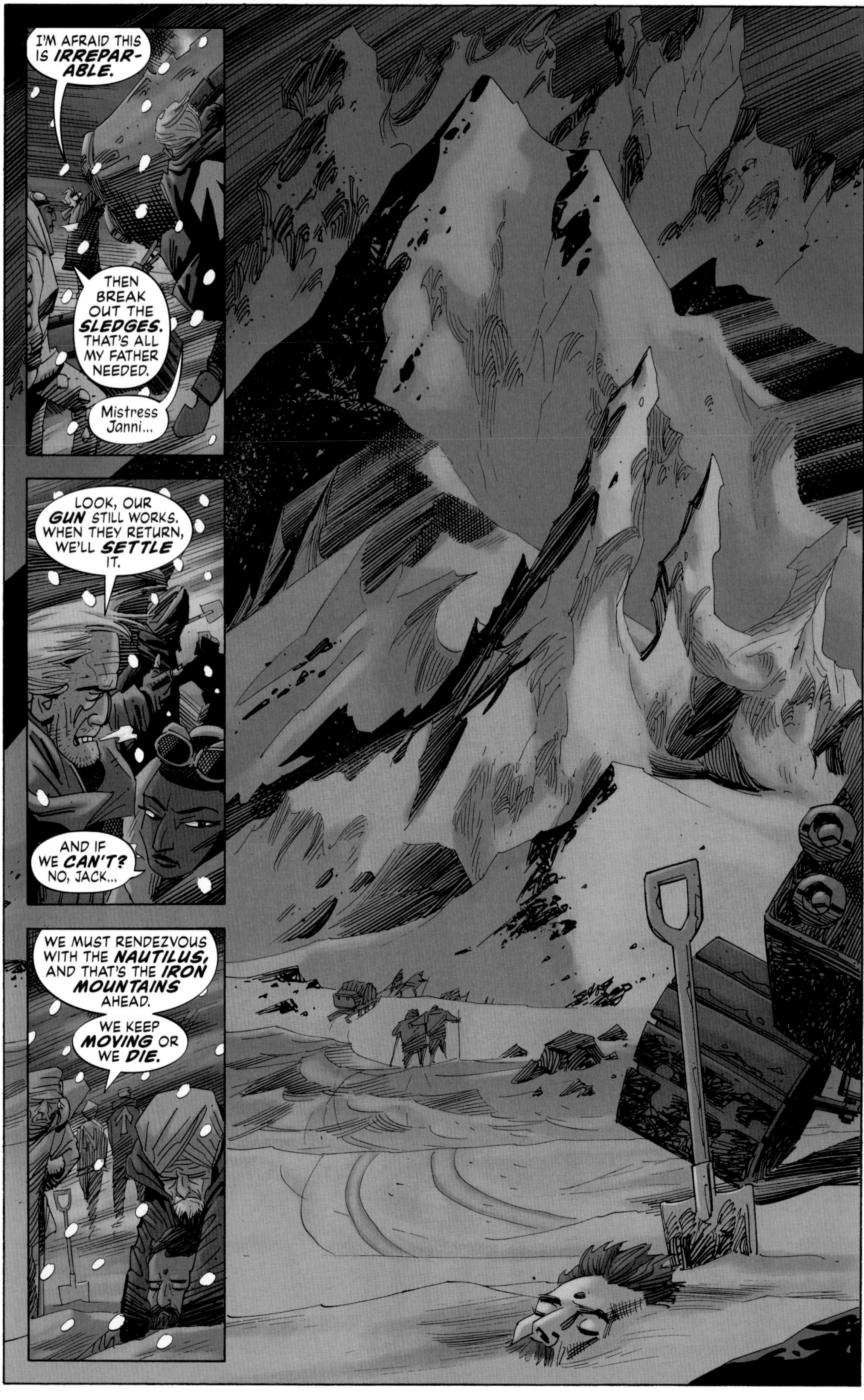
I'M AFRAID THIS IS IRREPARABLE.
THEN BREAK OUT THE SLEDGES. THAT'S ALL MY FATHER NEEDED.
Mistress Janni...
LOOK, OUR GUN STILL WORKS. WHEN THEY RETURN, WE'LL SETTLE IT.
AND IF WE CAN'T? NO, JACK...
WE MUST RENDEZVOUS WITH THE NAUTILUS, AND THAT'S THE IRON MOUNTAINS AHEAD.
WE KEEP MOVING OR WE DIE.

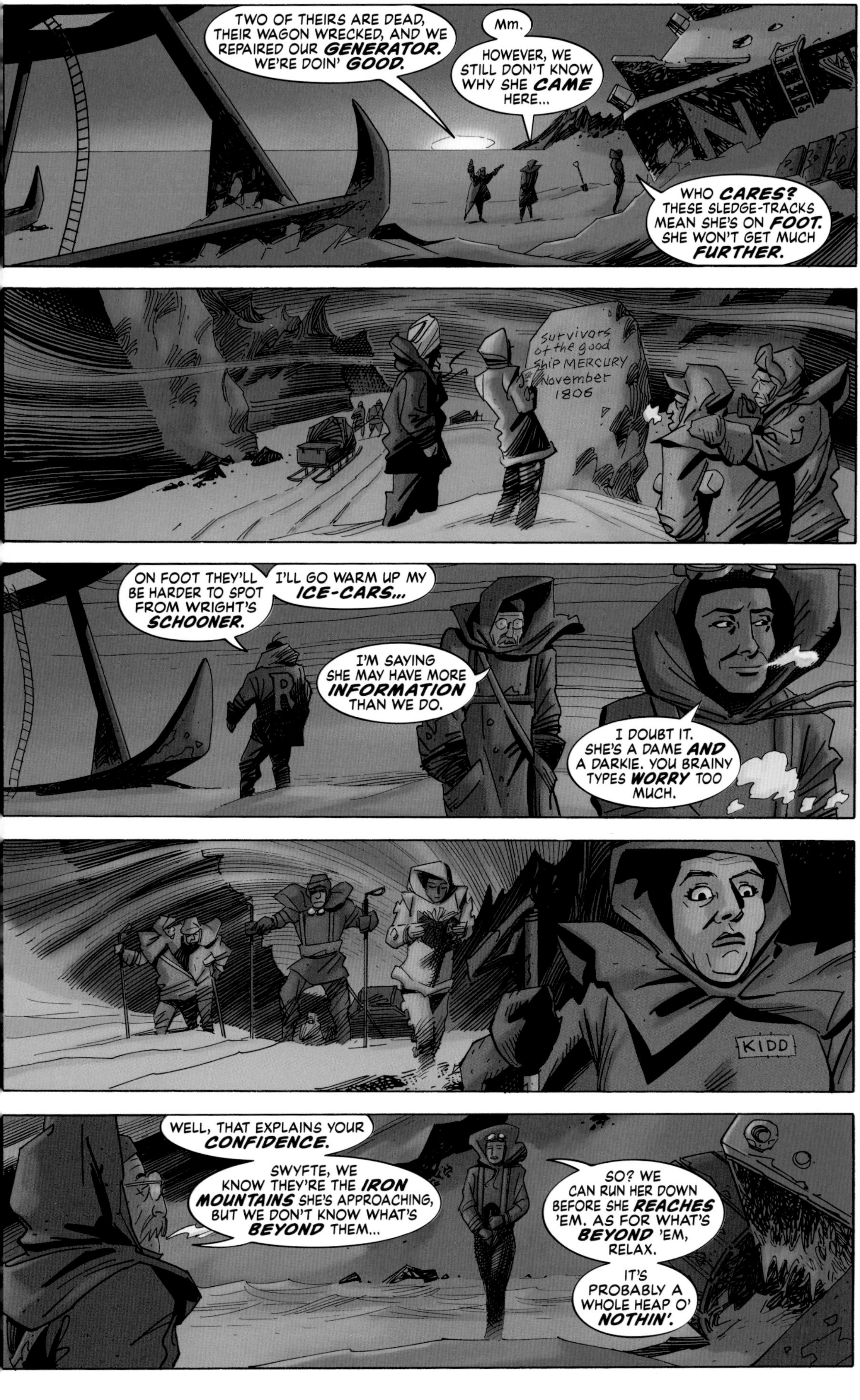
TWO OF THEIRS ARE DEAD, THEIR WAGON WRECKED, AND WE REPAIRED OUR GENERATOR. WE'RE DOIN' GOOD.
Mm.
HOWEVER, WE STILL DON'T KNOW WHY SHE CAME HERE...
WHO CARES? THESE SLEDGE-TRACKS MEAN SHE'S ON FOOT. SHE WON'T GET MUCH FURTHER.
Survivors of the good ship MERCURY November 1806
ON FOOT THEY'LL BE HARDER TO SPOT FROM WRIGHT'S SCHOONER.
I'LL GO WARM UP MY ICE-CARS...
I'M SAYING SHE MAY HAVE MORE INFORMATION THAN WE DO.
I DOUBT IT. SHE'S A DAME AND A DARKIE. YOU BRAINY TYPES WORRY TOO MUCH.
KIDD
WELL, THAT EXPLAINS YOUR CONFIDENCE.
SWYFTE, WE KNOW THEY'RE THE IRON MOUNTAINS SHE'S APPROACHING, BUT WE DON'T KNOW WHAT'S BEYOND THEM...
SO? WE CAN RUN HER DOWN BEFORE SHE REACHES 'EM. AS FOR WHAT'S BEYOND 'EM, RELAX.
IT'S PROBABLY A WHOLE HEAP O' NOTHIN'.

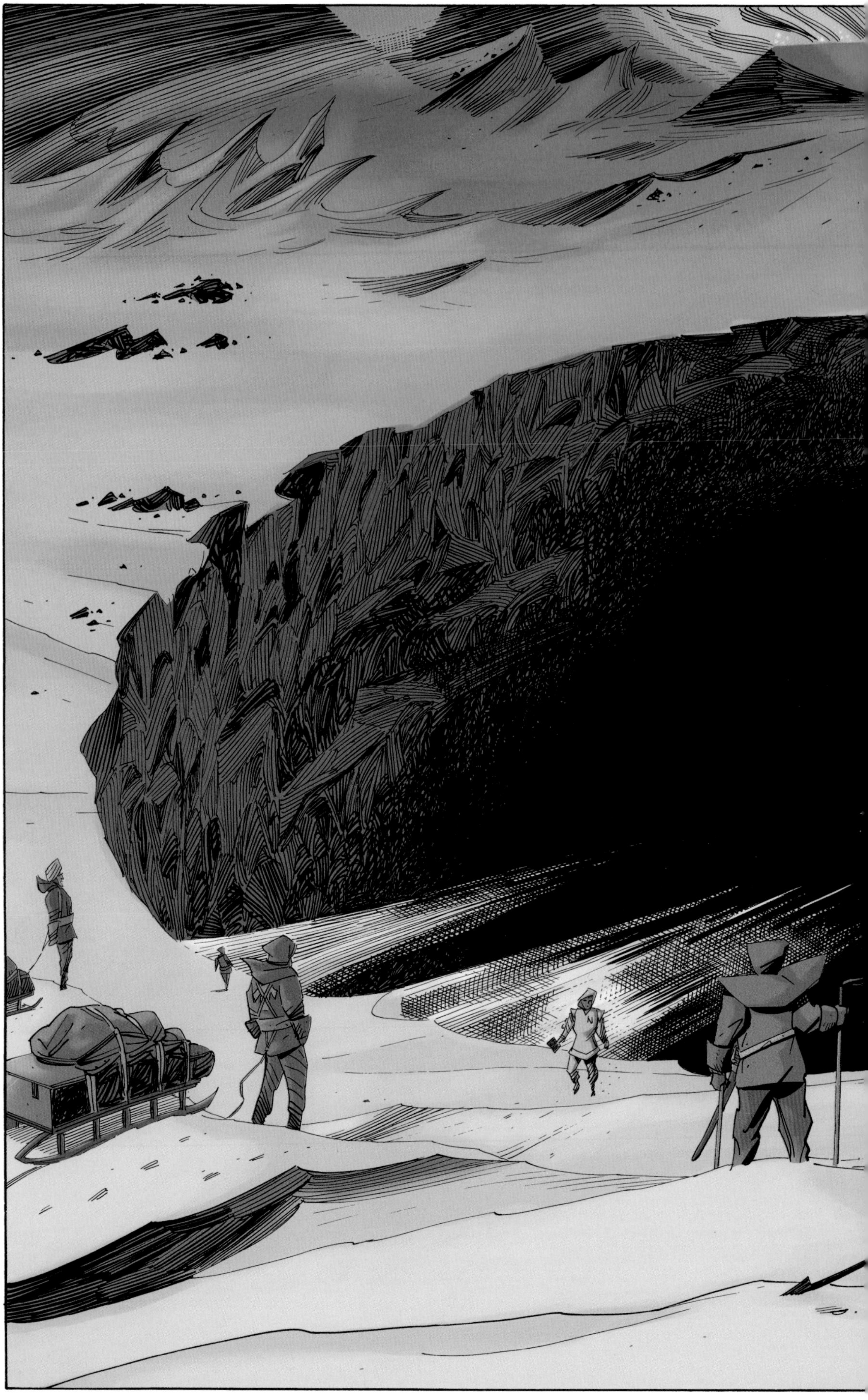

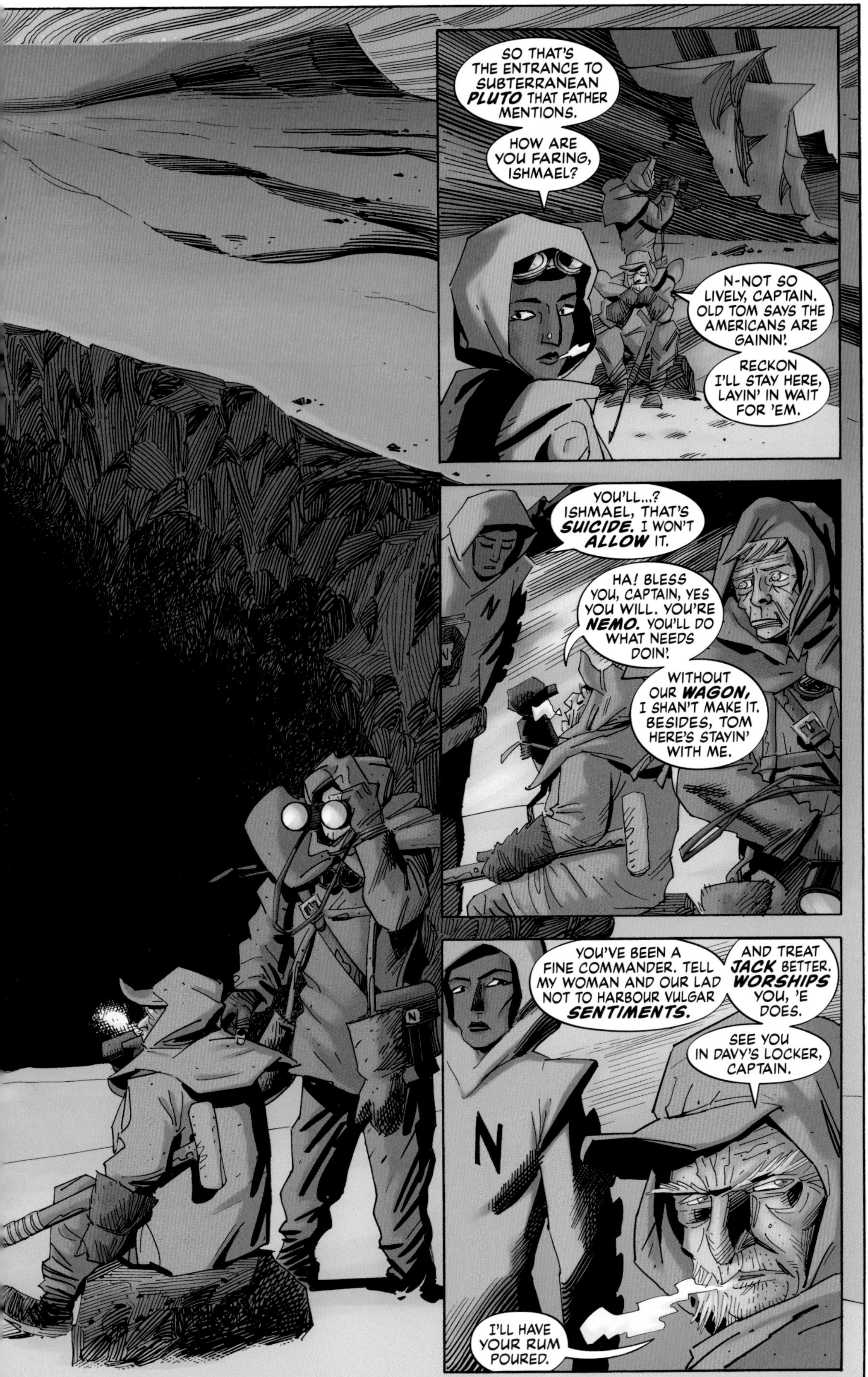
SO THAT'S THE ENTRANCE TO SUBTERRANEAN PLUTO THAT FATHER MENTIONS.
HOW ARE YOU FARING, ISHMAEL?
N-NOT SO LIVELY, CAPTAIN. OLD TOM SAYS THE AMERICANS ARE GAININ'.
RECKON I'LL STAY HERE, LAYIN' IN WAIT FOR 'EM.
YOU'LL...? ISHMAEL, THAT'S SUICIDE. I WON'T ALLOW IT.
HA! BLESS YOU, CAPTAIN, YES YOU WILL. YOU'RE NEMO. YOU'LL DO WHAT NEEDS DOIN'.
WITHOUT OUR WAGON, I SHAN'T MAKE IT. BESIDES, TOM HERE'S STAYIN' WITH ME.
YOU'VE BEEN A FINE COMMANDER. TELL MY WOMAN AND OUR LAD NOT TO HARBOUR VULGAR SENTIMENTS.
AND TREAT JACK BETTER. JACK WORSHIPS YOU, 'E DOES.
SEE YOU IN DAVY'S LOCKER, CAPTAIN.
I'LL HAVE YOUR RUM POURED.

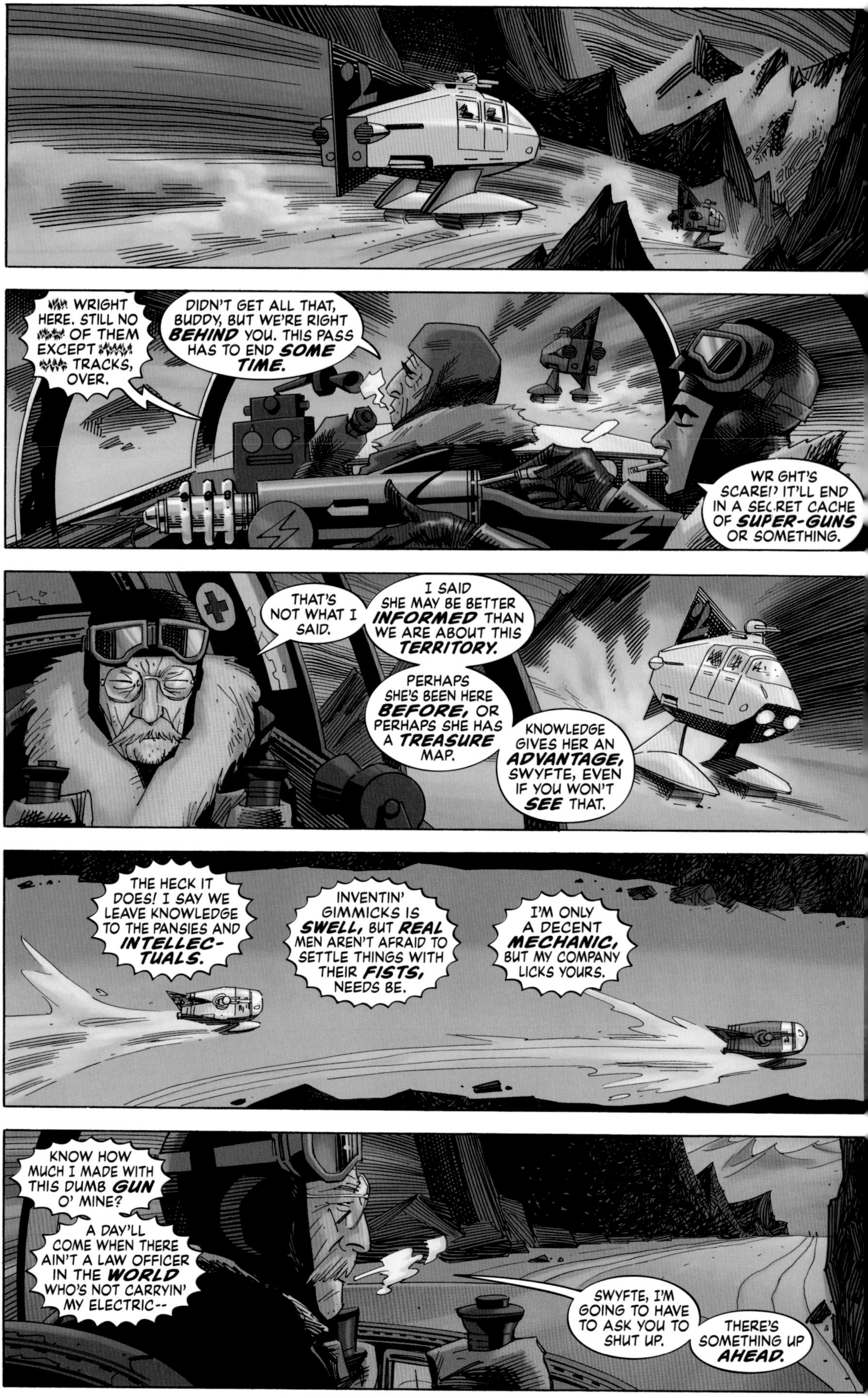
WRIGHT HERE. STILL NO OF THEM EXCEPT TRACKS, OVER.
DIDN'T GET ALL THAT, BUDDY, BUT WE'RE RIGHT BEHIND YOU. THIS PASS HAS TO END SOME TIME.
WR GHT'S SCARED IT'LL END IN A SECRET CACHE OF SUPER-GUNS OR SOMETHING.
THAT'S NOT WHAT I SAID.
I SAID SHE MAY BE BETTER INFORMED THAN WE ARE ABOUT THIS TERRITORY.
PERHAPS SHE'S BEEN HERE BEFORE, OR PERHAPS SHE HAS A TREASURE MAP.
KNOWLEDGE GIVES HER AN ADVANTAGE, SWYFTE, EVEN IF YOU WON'T SEE THAT.
THE HECK IT DOES! I SAY WE LEAVE KNOWLEDGE TO THE PANSIES AND INTELLEC-TUALS.
INVENTIN' GIMMICKS IS SWELL, BUT REAL MEN AREN'T AFRAID TO SETTLE THINGS WITH THEIR FISTS, NEEDS BE.
I'M ONLY A DECENT MECHANIC, BUT MY COMPANY LICKS YOURS.
KNOW HOW MUCH I MADE WITH THIS DUMB GUN O' MINE?
A DAY'LL COME WHEN THERE AIN'T A LAW OFFICER IN THE WORLD WHO'S NOT CARRYIN' MY ELECTRIC--
SWYFTE, I'M GOING TO HAVE TO ASK YOU TO SHUT UP.
THERE'S SOMETHING UP AHEAD.

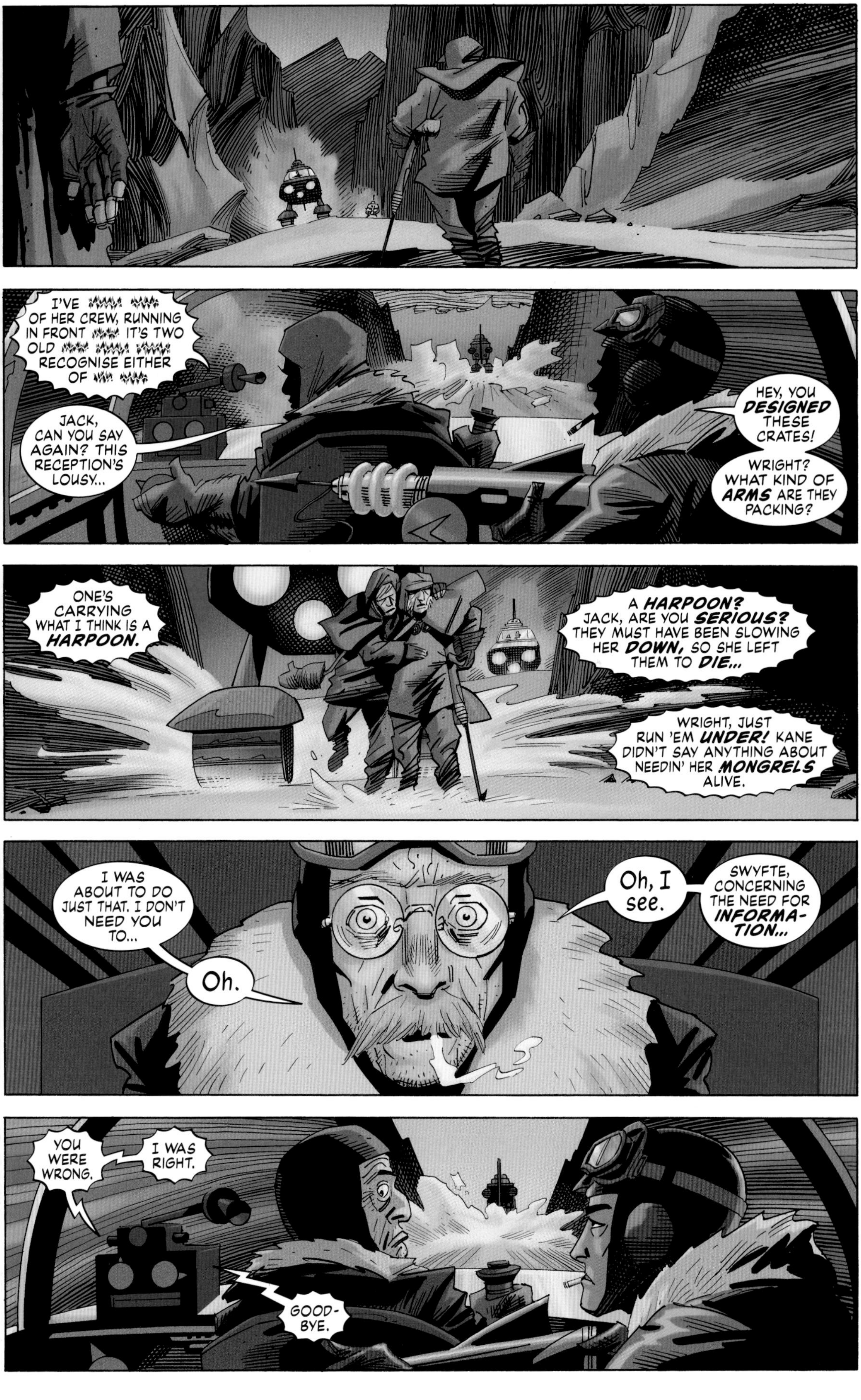

I'VE OF HER CREW, RUNNING IN FRONT IT'S TWO OLD RECOGNISE EITHER OF
JACK, CAN YOU SAY AGAIN? THIS RECEPTION'S LOUSY...
HEY, YOU DESIGNED THESE CRATES!
WRIGHT? WHAT KIND OF ARMS ARE THEY PACKING?
ONE'S CARRYING WHAT I THINK IS A HARPOON.
A HARPOON? JACK, ARE YOU SERIOUS? THEY MUST HAVE BEEN SLOWING HER DOWN, SO SHE LEFT THEM TO DIE...
WRIGHT, JUST RUN 'EM UNDER! KANE DIDN'T SAY ANYTHING ABOUT NEEDIN' HER MONGRELS ALIVE.
I WAS ABOUT TO DO JUST THAT. I DON'T NEED YOU TO...
Oh.
Oh, I see.
SWYFTE, CONCERNING THE NEED FOR INFORMATION...
YOU WERE WRONG.
I WAS RIGHT.
GOOD-BYE.

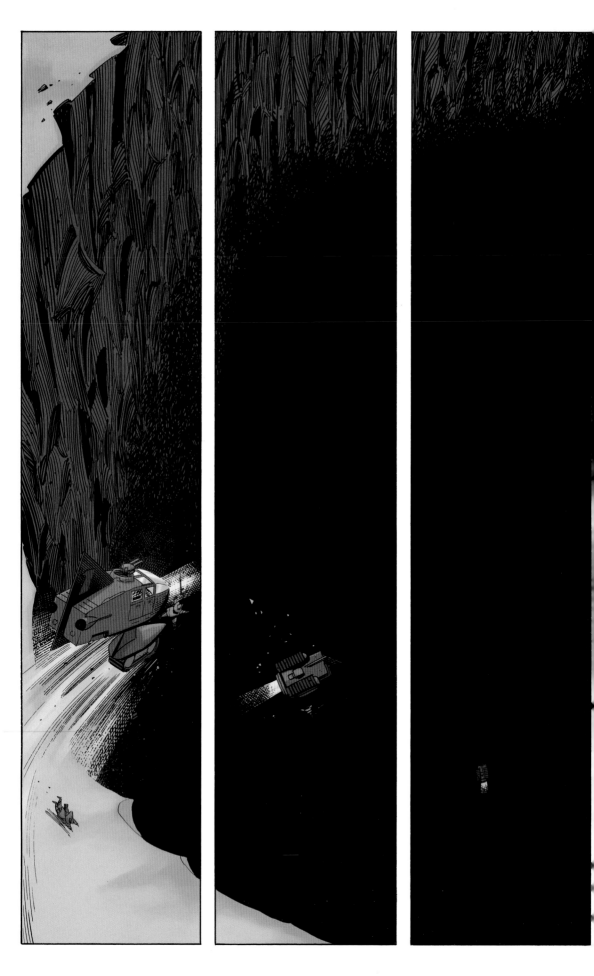

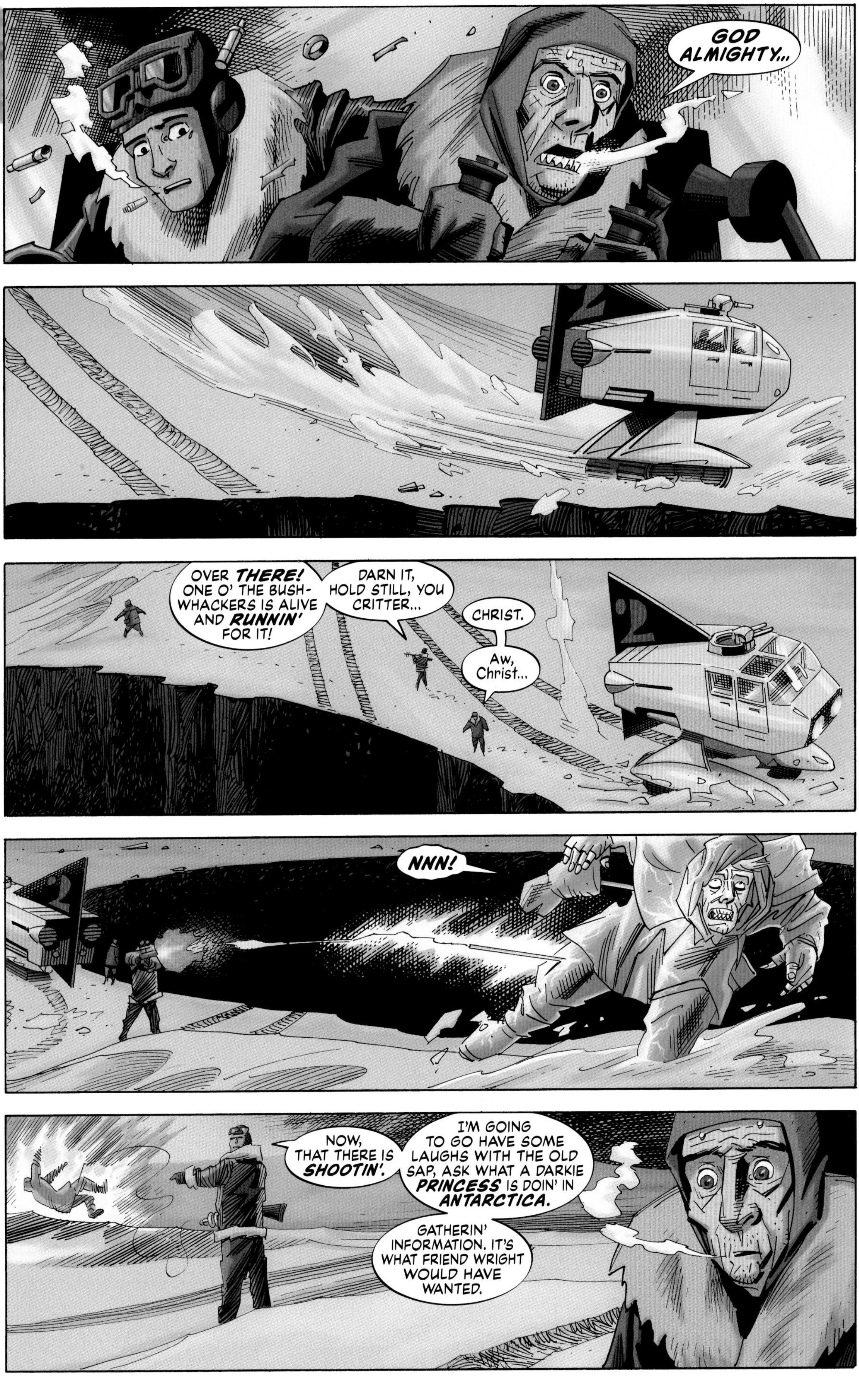
GOD ALMIGHTY...
OVER THERE! ONE O' THE BUSH-WHACKERS IS ALIVE AND RUNNIN' FOR IT!
DARN IT, HOLD STILL, YOU CRITTER...
CHRIST.
Aw, Christ...
NNN!
NOW, THAT THERE IS SHOOTIN'.
I'M GOING TO GO HAVE SOME LAUGHS WITH THE OLD SAP, ASK WHAT A DARKIE PRINCESS IS DOIN' IN ANTARCTICA.
GATHERIN' INFORMATION. IT'S WHAT FRIEND WRIGHT WOULD HAVE WANTED.

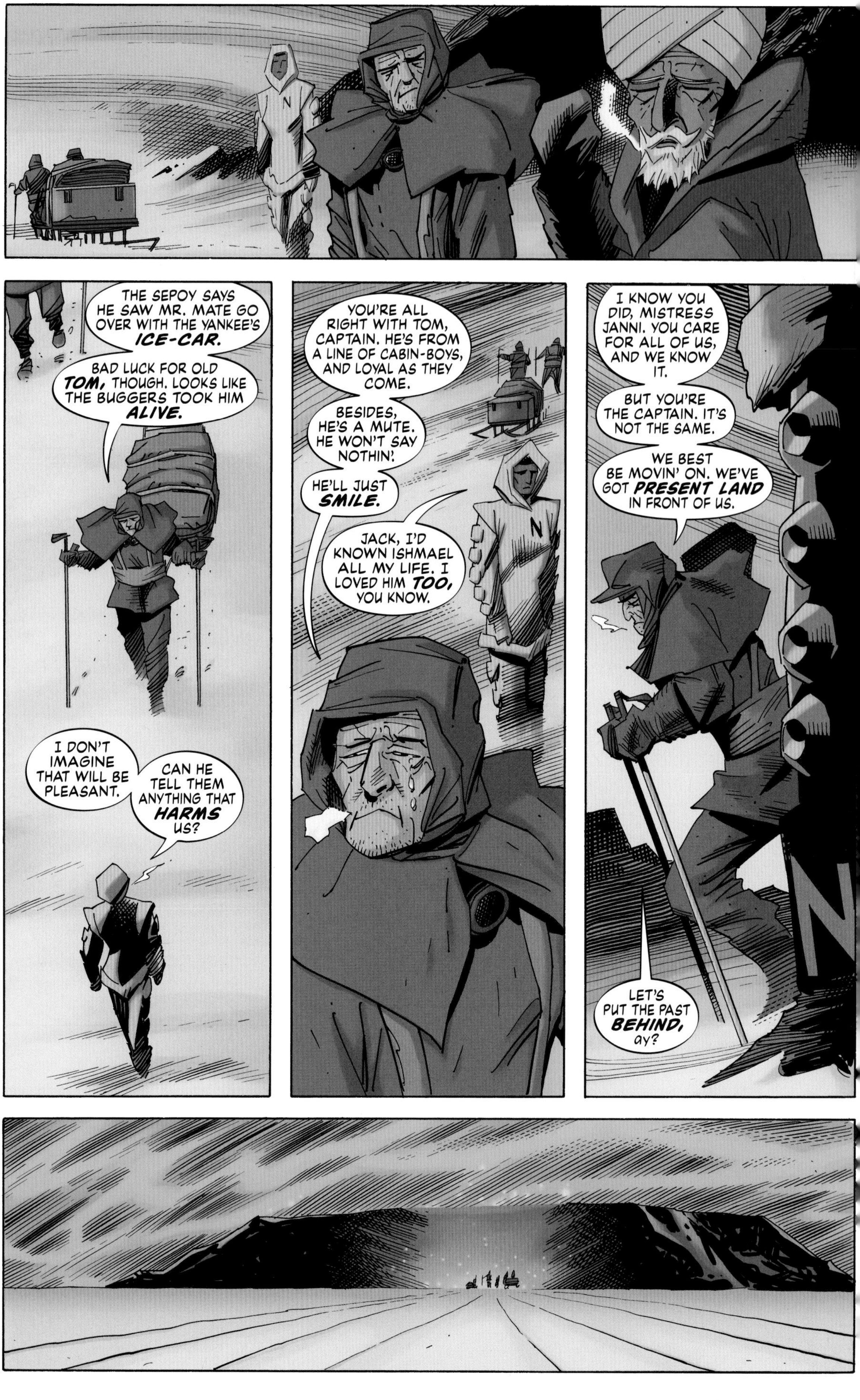
THE SEPOY SAYS HE SAW MR. MATE GO OVER WITH THE YANKEE'S ICE-CAR.
BAD LUCK FOR OLD TOM, THOUGH. LOOKS LIKE THE BUGGERS TOOK HIM ALIVE.
I DON'T IMAGINE THAT WILL BE PLEASANT.
CAN HE TELL THEM ANYTHING THAT HARMS US?
YOU'RE ALL RIGHT WITH TOM, CAPTAIN. HE'S FROM A LINE OF CABIN-BOYS, AND LOYAL AS THEY COME.
BESIDES, HE'S A MUTE. HE WON'T SAY NOTHIN'.
HE'LL JUST SMILE.
JACK, I'D KNOWN ISHMAEL ALL MY LIFE. I LOVED HIM TOO, YOU KNOW.
I KNOW YOU DID, MISTRESS JANNI. YOU CARE FOR ALL OF US, AND WE KNOW IT.
BUT YOU'RE THE CAPTAIN. IT'S NOT THE SAME.
WE BEST BE MOVIN' ON. WE'VE GOT PRESENT LAND IN FRONT OF US.
LET'S PUT THE PAST BEHIND, ay?

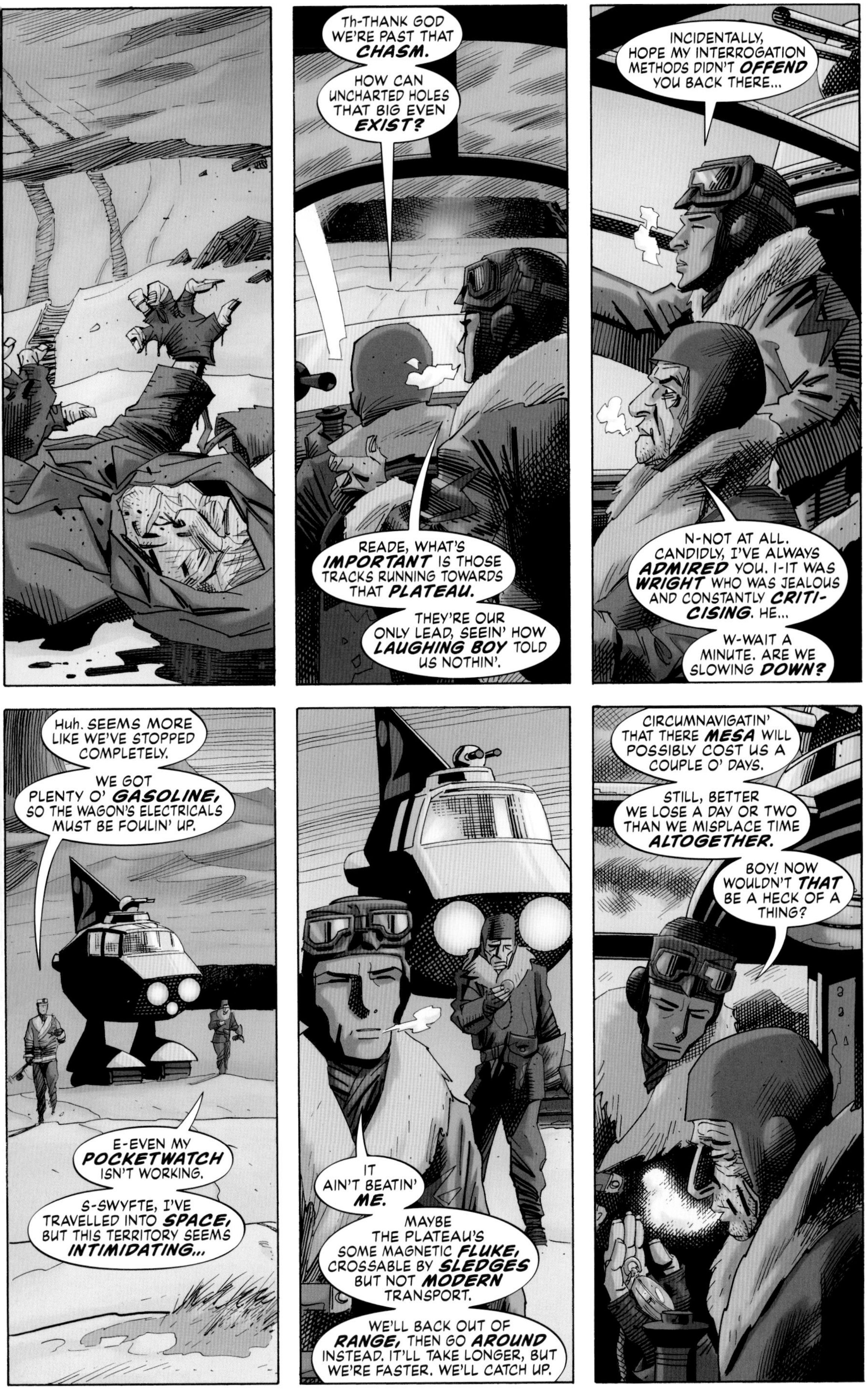
Th-THANK GOD WE'RE PAST THAT CHASM.
HOW CAN UNCHARTED HOLES THAT BIG EVEN EXIST?
READE, WHAT'S IMPORTANT IS THOSE TRACKS RUNNING TOWARDS THAT PLATEAU.
THEY'RE OUR ONLY LEAD, SEEIN' HOW LAUGHING BOY TOLD US NOTHIN'.
INCIDENTALLY, HOPE MY INTERROGATION METHODS DIDN'T OFFEND YOU BACK THERE...
N-NOT AT ALL. CANDIDLY, I'VE ALWAYS ADMIRED YOU. I-IT WAS WRIGHT WHO WAS JEALOUS AND CONSTANTLY CRITI-CISING. HE...
W-WAIT A MINUTE. ARE WE SLOWING DOWN?
Huh. SEEMS MORE LIKE WE'VE STOPPED COMPLETELY.
WE GOT PLENTY O' GASOLINE, SO THE WAGON'S ELECTRICALS MUST BE FOULIN' UP.
E-EVEN MY POCKETWATCH ISN'T WORKING.
S-SWYFTE, I'VE TRAVELLED INTO SPACE, BUT THIS TERRITORY SEEMS INTIMIDATING...
IT AIN'T BEATIN' ME.
MAYBE THE PLATEAU'S SOME MAGNETIC FLUKE, CROSSABLE BY SLEDGES BUT NOT MODERN TRANSPORT.
WE'LL BACK OUT OF RANGE, THEN GO AROUND INSTEAD. IT'LL TAKE LONGER, BUT WE'RE FASTER. WE'LL CATCH UP.
CIRCUMNAVIGATIN' THAT THERE MESA WILL POSSIBLY COST US A COUPLE O' DAYS.
STILL, BETTER WE LOSE A DAY OR TWO THAN WE MISPLACE TIME ALTOGETHER.
BOY! NOW WOULDN'T THAT BE A HECK OF A THING?

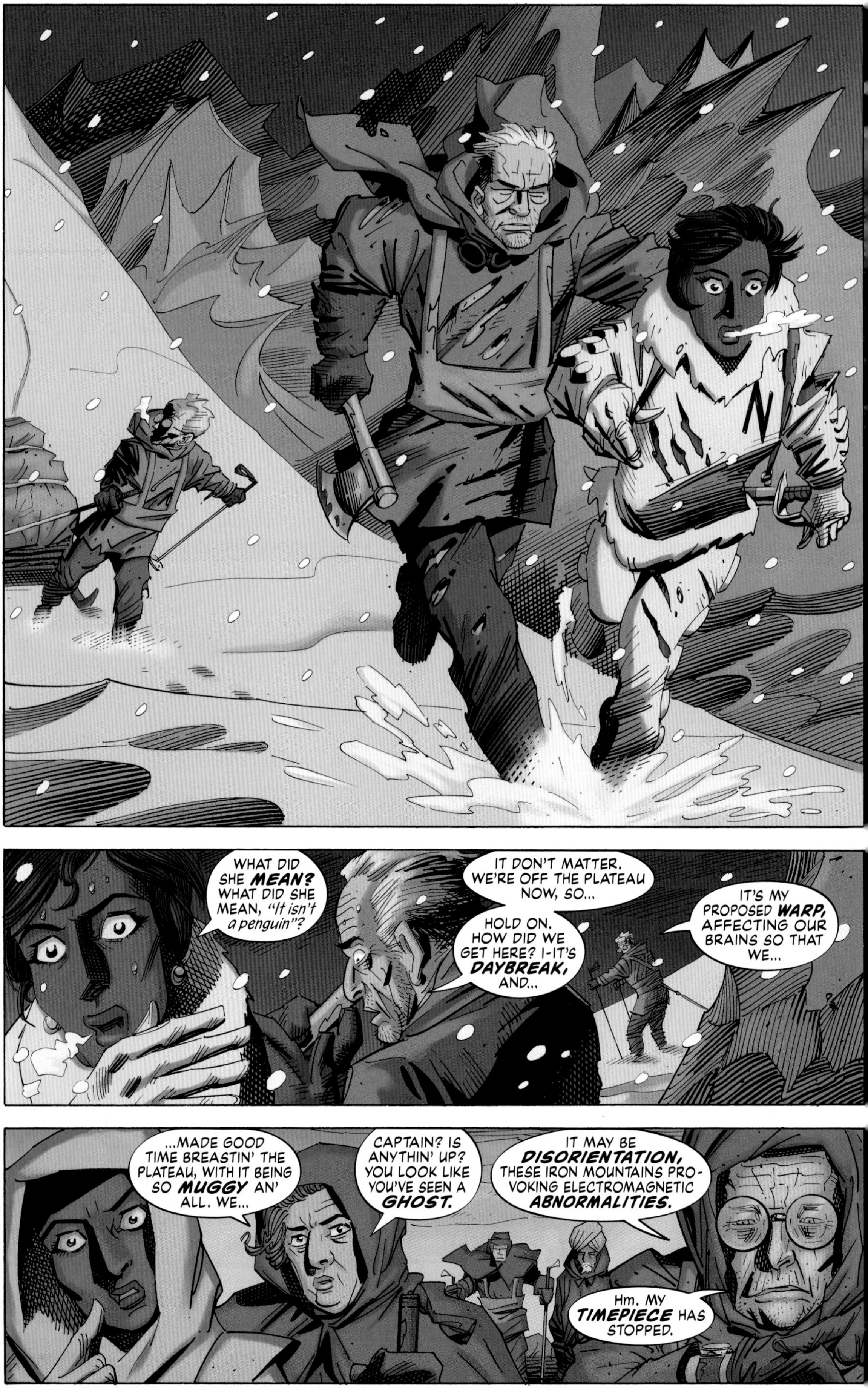
WHAT DID SHE *MEAN?* WHAT DID SHE MEAN, *"It isn't a penguin"?*
IT DON'T MATTER. WE'RE OFF THE PLATEAU NOW, SO...
HOLD ON. HOW DID WE GET HERE? I-IT'S *DAYBREAK,* AND...
IT'S MY PROPOSED *WARP,* AFFECTING OUR BRAINS SO THAT WE...
...MADE GOOD TIME BREASTIN' THE PLATEAU, WITH IT BEING SO *MUGGY* AN' ALL. WE...
CAPTAIN? IS ANYTHIN' UP? YOU LOOK LIKE YOU'VE SEEN A *GHOST.*
IT MAY BE *DISORIENTATION,* THESE IRON MOUNTAINS PRO-VOKING ELECTROMAGNETIC *ABNORMALITIES.*
Hm. MY *TIMEPIECE* HAS STOPPED.

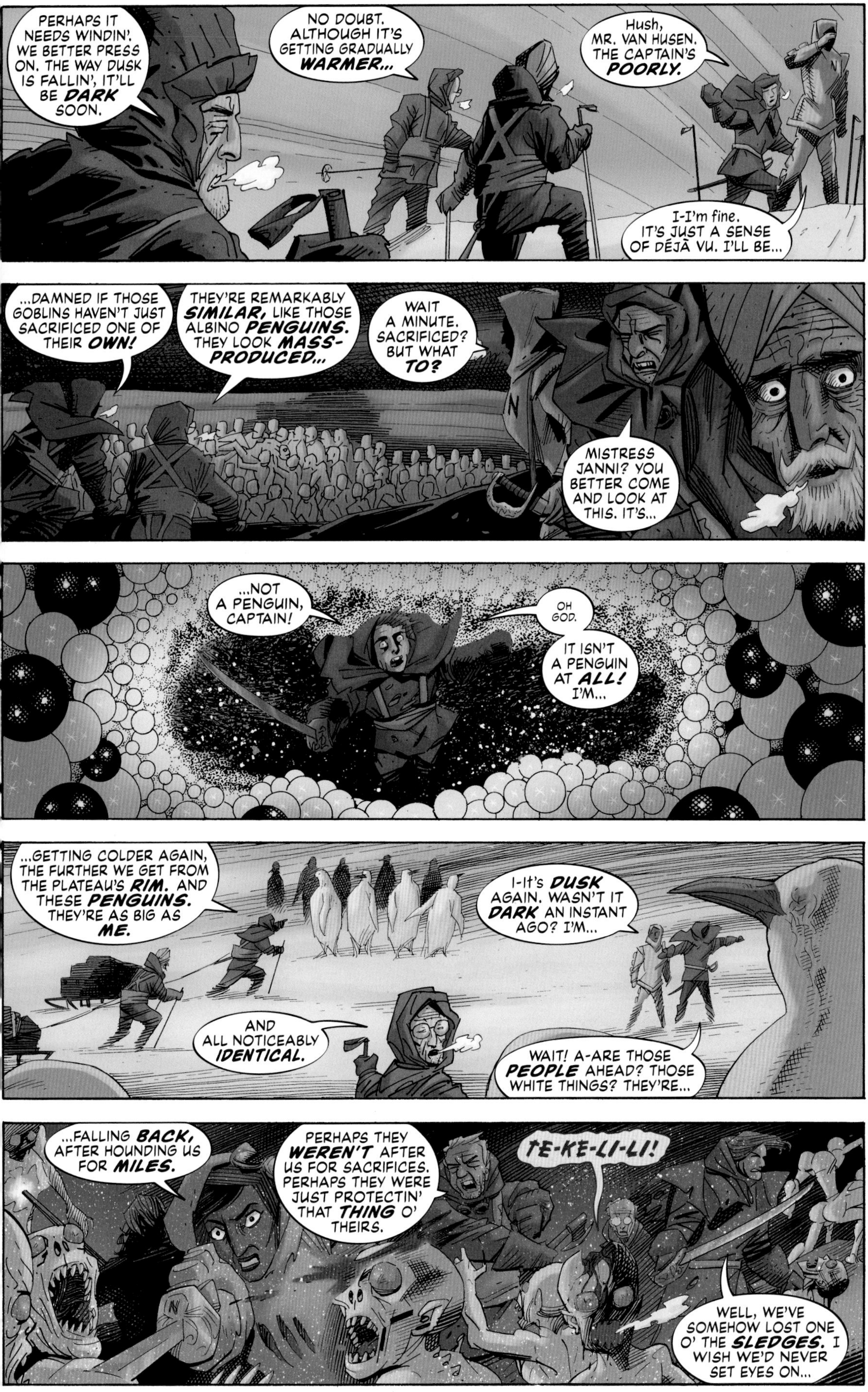
PERHAPS IT NEEDS WINDIN'. WE BETTER PRESS ON. THE WAY DUSK IS FALLIN', IT'LL BE DARK SOON.
NO DOUBT. ALTHOUGH IT'S GETTING GRADUALLY WARMER...
Hush, MR. VAN HUSEN. THE CAPTAIN'S POORLY.
I-I'm fine. IT'S JUST A SENSE OF DÉJÃ VU. I'LL BE...
...DAMNED IF THOSE GOBLINS HAVEN'T JUST SACRIFICED ONE OF THEIR OWN!
THEY'RE REMARKABLY SIMILAR, LIKE THOSE ALBINO PENGUINS. THEY LOOK MASS-PRODUCED...
WAIT A MINUTE. SACRIFICED? BUT WHAT TO?
MISTRESS JANNI? YOU BETTER COME AND LOOK AT THIS. IT'S...
...NOT A PENGUIN, CAPTAIN!
OH GOD.
IT ISN'T A PENGUIN AT ALL! I'M...
...GETTING COLDER AGAIN, THE FURTHER WE GET FROM THE PLATEAU'S RIM. AND THESE PENGUINS. THEY'RE AS BIG AS ME.
I-It's DUSK AGAIN. WASN'T IT DARK AN INSTANT AGO? I'M...
AND ALL NOTICEABLY IDENTICAL.
WAIT! A-ARE THOSE PEOPLE AHEAD? THOSE WHITE THINGS? THEY'RE...
...FALLING BACK, AFTER HOUNDING US FOR MILES.
PERHAPS THEY WEREN'T AFTER US FOR SACRIFICES. PERHAPS THEY WERE JUST PROTECTIN' THAT THING O' THEIRS.
TE-KE-LI-LI!
WELL, WE'VE SOMEHOW LOST ONE O' THE SLEDGES. I WISH WE'D NEVER SET EYES ON...

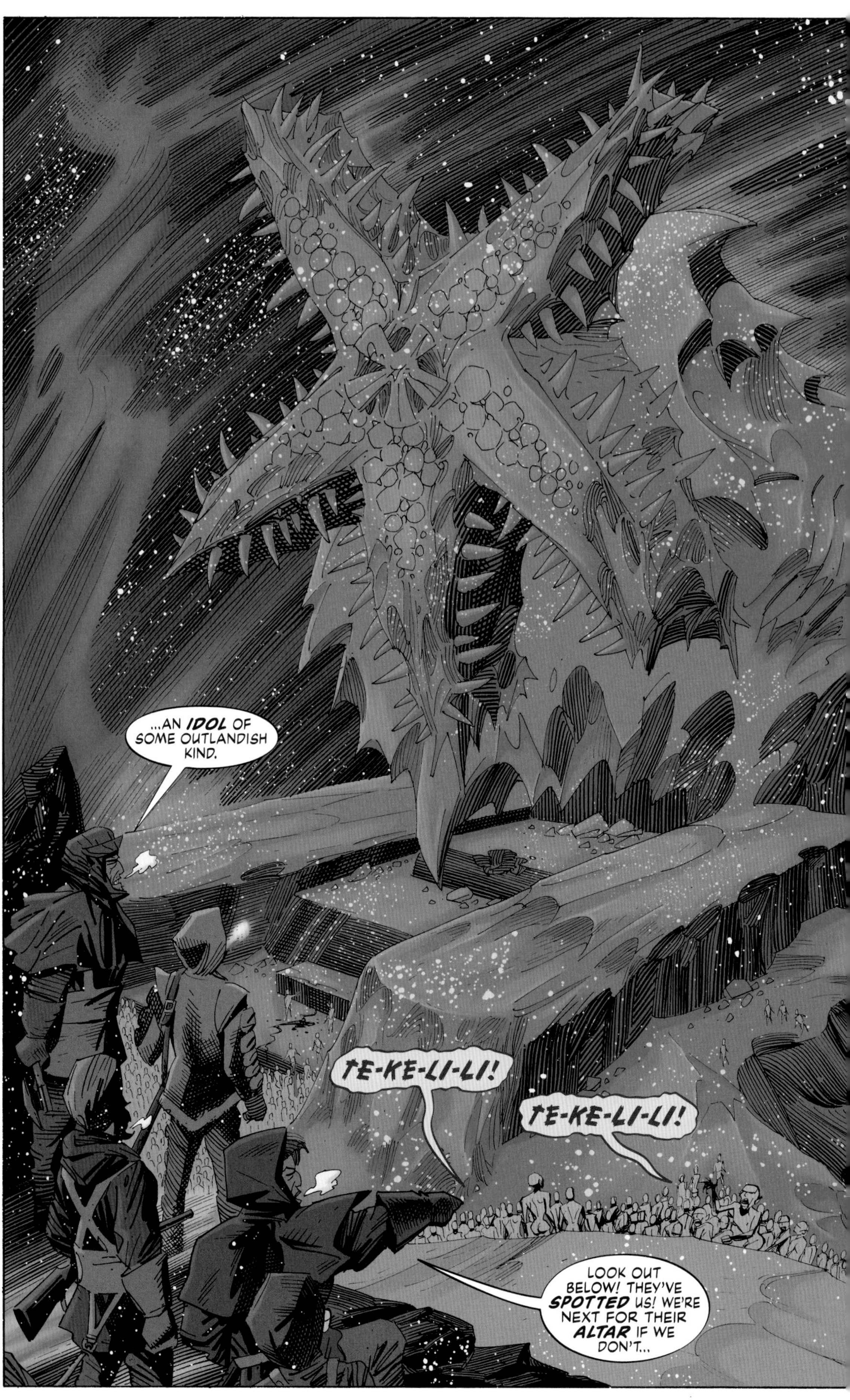
...AN IDOL OF SOME OUTLANDISH KIND.
TE-KE-LI-LI!
TE-KE-LI-LI!
LOOK OUT BELOW! THEY'VE SPOTTED US! WE'RE NEXT FOR THEIR ALTAR IF WE DON'T...

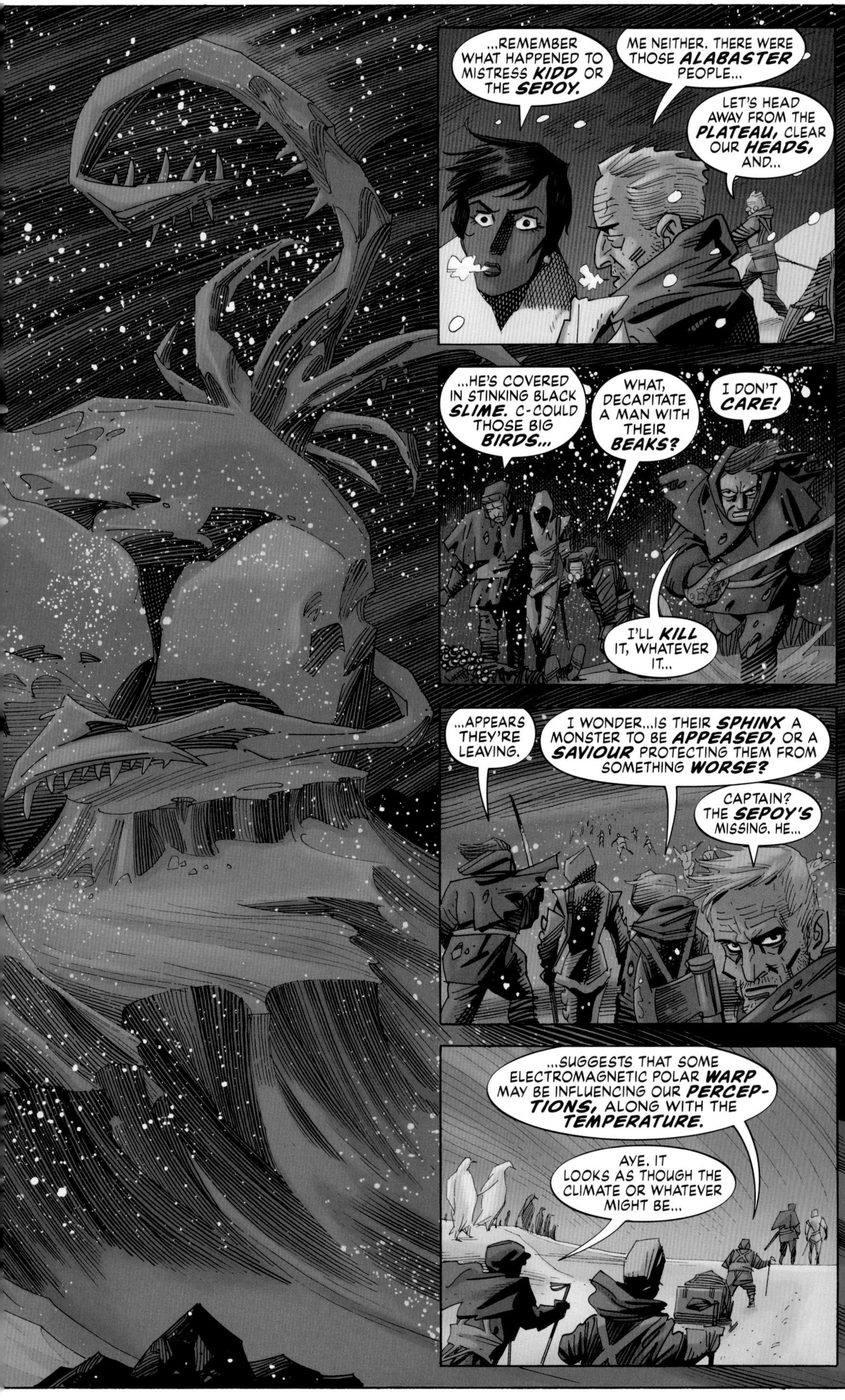
...REMEMBER WHAT HAPPENED TO MISTRESS KIDD OR THE SEPOY.
ME NEITHER. THERE WERE THOSE ALABASTER PEOPLE...
LET'S HEAD AWAY FROM THE PLATEAU, CLEAR OUR HEADS, AND...
...HE'S COVERED IN STINKING BLACK SLIME. C-COULD THOSE BIG BIRDS...
WHAT, DECAPITATE A MAN WITH THEIR BEAKS?
I DON'T CARE!
I'LL KILL IT, WHATEVER IT...
...APPEARS THEY'RE LEAVING.
I WONDER...IS THEIR SPHINX A MONSTER TO BE APPEASED, OR A SAVIOUR PROTECTING THEM FROM SOMETHING WORSE?
CAPTAIN? THE SEPOY'S MISSING. HE...
...SUGGESTS THAT SOME ELECTROMAGNETIC POLAR WARP MAY BE INFLUENCING OUR PERCEP-TIONS, ALONG WITH THE TEMPERATURE.
AYE. IT LOOKS AS THOUGH THE CLIMATE OR WHATEVER MIGHT BE...

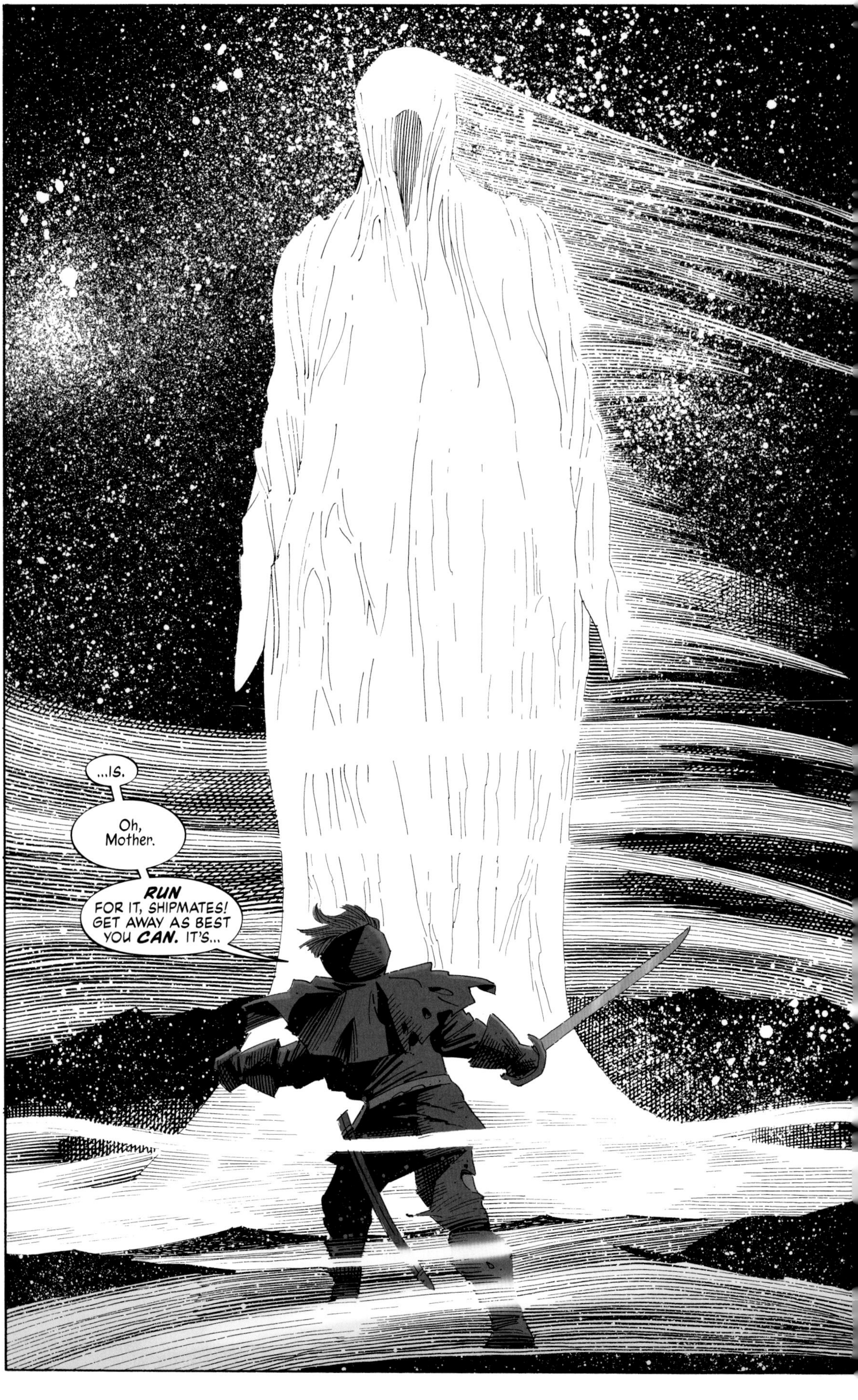
...IS.
Oh, Mother.
RUN FOR IT, SHIPMATES! GET AWAY AS BEST YOU CAN. IT'S...

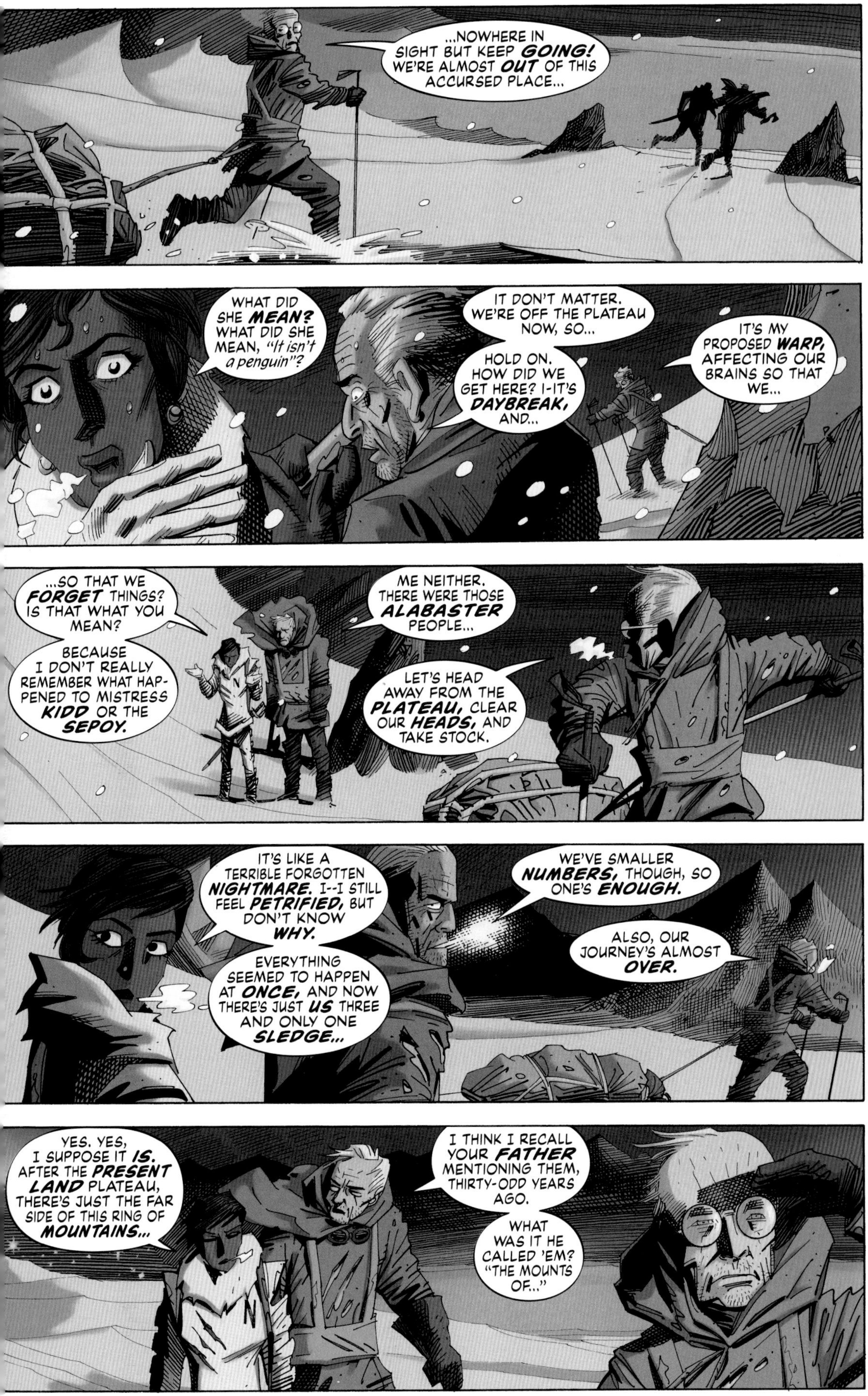
...NOWHERE IN SIGHT BUT KEEP GOING! WE'RE ALMOST OUT OF THIS ACCURSED PLACE...
WHAT DID SHE MEAN? WHAT DID SHE MEAN, "It isn't a penguin"?
IT DON'T MATTER. WE'RE OFF THE PLATEAU NOW, SO...
HOLD ON. HOW DID WE GET HERE? I-IT'S DAYBREAK, AND...
IT'S MY PROPOSED WARP, AFFECTING OUR BRAINS SO THAT WE...
...SO THAT WE FORGET THINGS? IS THAT WHAT YOU MEAN?
BECAUSE I DON'T REALLY REMEMBER WHAT HAPPENED TO MISTRESS KIDD OR THE SEPOY.
ME NEITHER. THERE WERE THOSE ALABASTER PEOPLE...
LET'S HEAD AWAY FROM THE PLATEAU, CLEAR OUR HEADS, AND TAKE STOCK.
IT'S LIKE A TERRIBLE FORGOTTEN NIGHTMARE. I--I STILL FEEL PETRIFIED, BUT DON'T KNOW WHY.
EVERYTHING SEEMED TO HAPPEN AT ONCE, AND NOW THERE'S JUST US THREE AND ONLY ONE SLEDGE...
WE'VE SMALLER NUMBERS, THOUGH, SO ONE'S ENOUGH.
ALSO, OUR JOURNEY'S ALMOST OVER.
YES. YES, I SUPPOSE IT IS. AFTER THE PRESENT LAND PLATEAU, THERE'S JUST THE FAR SIDE OF THIS RING OF MOUNTAINS...
I THINK I RECALL YOUR FATHER MENTIONING THEM, THIRTY-ODD YEARS AGO.
WHAT WAS IT HE CALLED 'EM? "THE MOUNTS OF..."

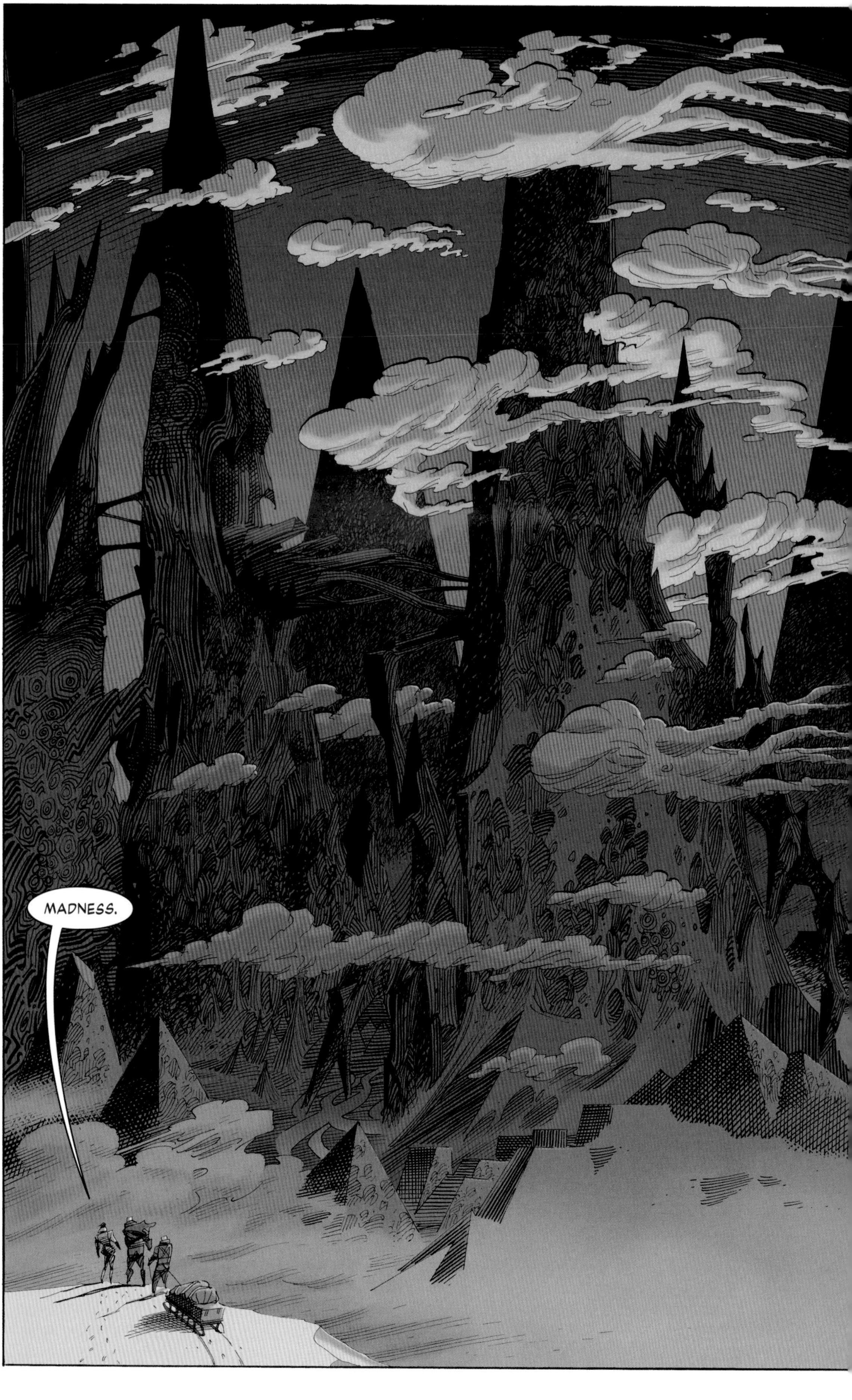
MADNESS.

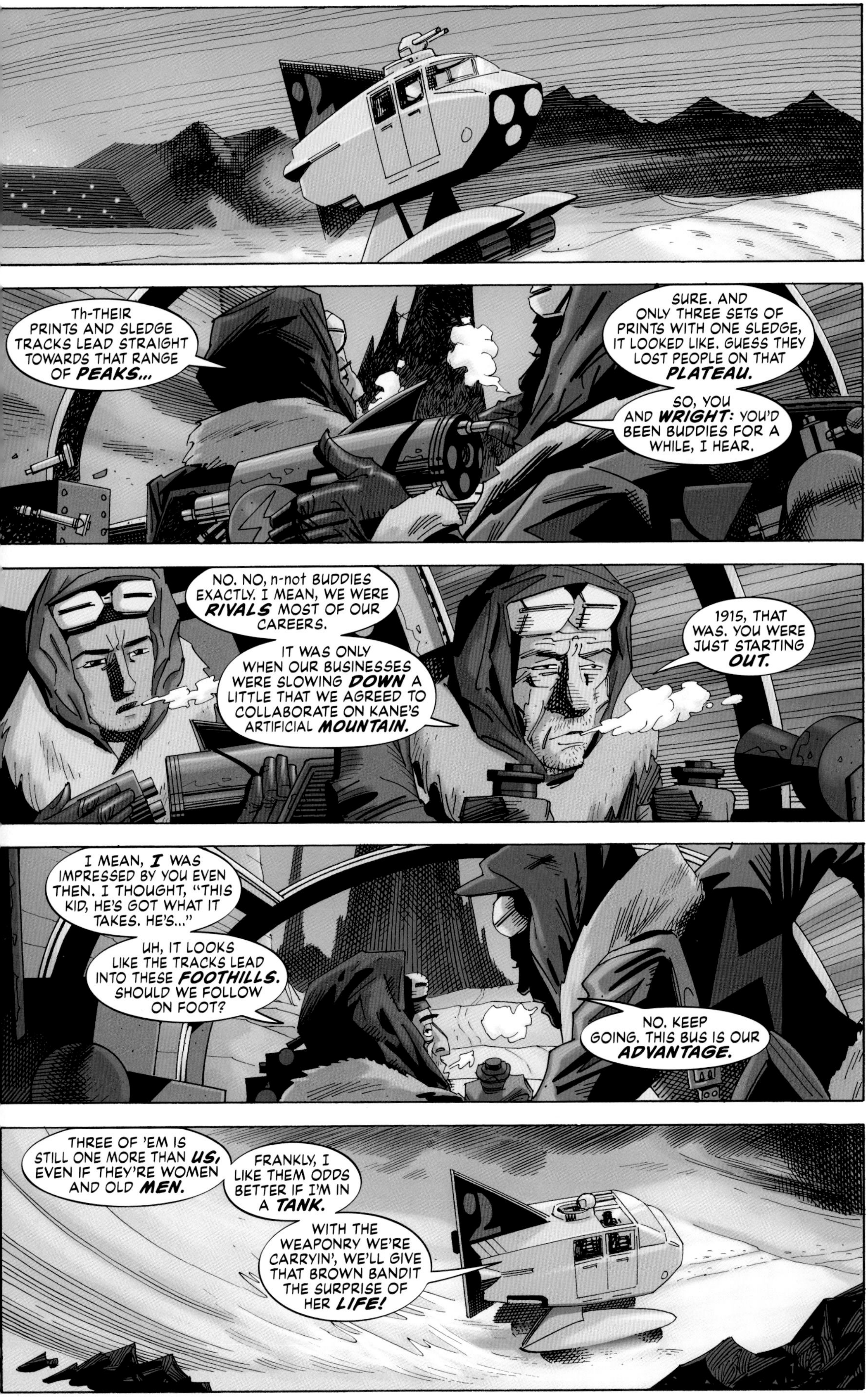
Th-THEIR PRINTS AND SLEDGE TRACKS LEAD STRAIGHT TOWARDS THAT RANGE OF PEAKS...
SURE. AND ONLY THREE SETS OF PRINTS WITH ONE SLEDGE, IT LOOKED LIKE. GUESS THEY LOST PEOPLE ON THAT PLATEAU.
SO, YOU AND WRIGHT: YOU'D BEEN BUDDIES FOR A WHILE, I HEAR.
NO. NO, n-not BUDDIES EXACTLY. I MEAN, WE WERE RIVALS MOST OF OUR CAREERS.
IT WAS ONLY WHEN OUR BUSINESSES WERE SLOWING DOWN A LITTLE THAT WE AGREED TO COLLABORATE ON KANE'S ARTIFICIAL MOUNTAIN.
1915, THAT WAS. YOU WERE JUST STARTING OUT.
I MEAN, I WAS IMPRESSED BY YOU EVEN THEN. I THOUGHT, "THIS KID, HE'S GOT WHAT IT TAKES. HE'S..."
UH, IT LOOKS LIKE THE TRACKS LEAD INTO THESE FOOTHILLS. SHOULD WE FOLLOW ON FOOT?
NO. KEEP GOING. THIS BUS IS OUR ADVANTAGE.
THREE OF 'EM IS STILL ONE MORE THAN US, EVEN IF THEY'RE WOMEN AND OLD MEN.
FRANKLY, I LIKE THEM ODDS BETTER IF I'M IN A TANK.
WITH THE WEAPONRY WE'RE CARRYIN', WE'LL GIVE THAT BROWN BANDIT THE SURPRISE OF HER LIFE!

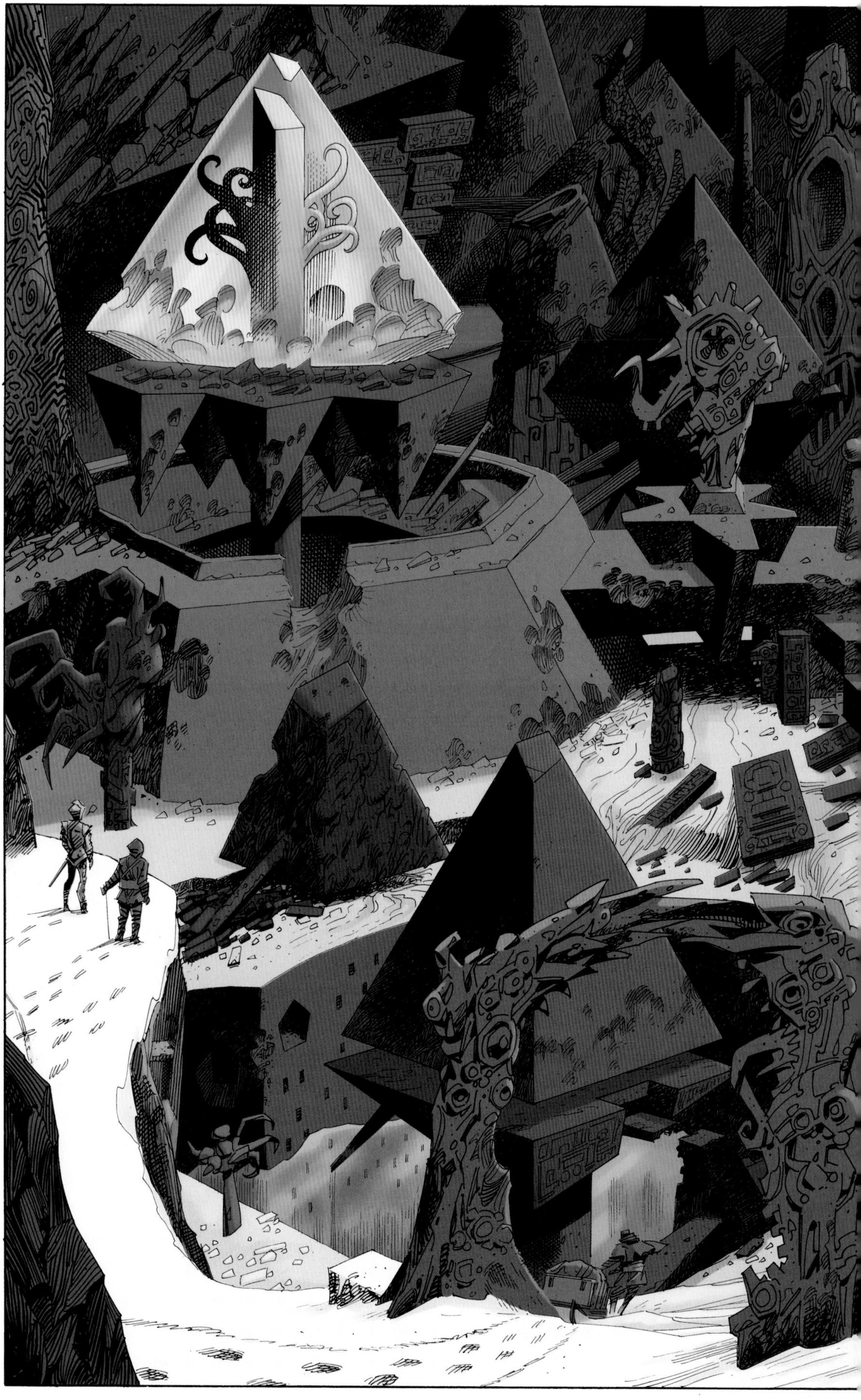

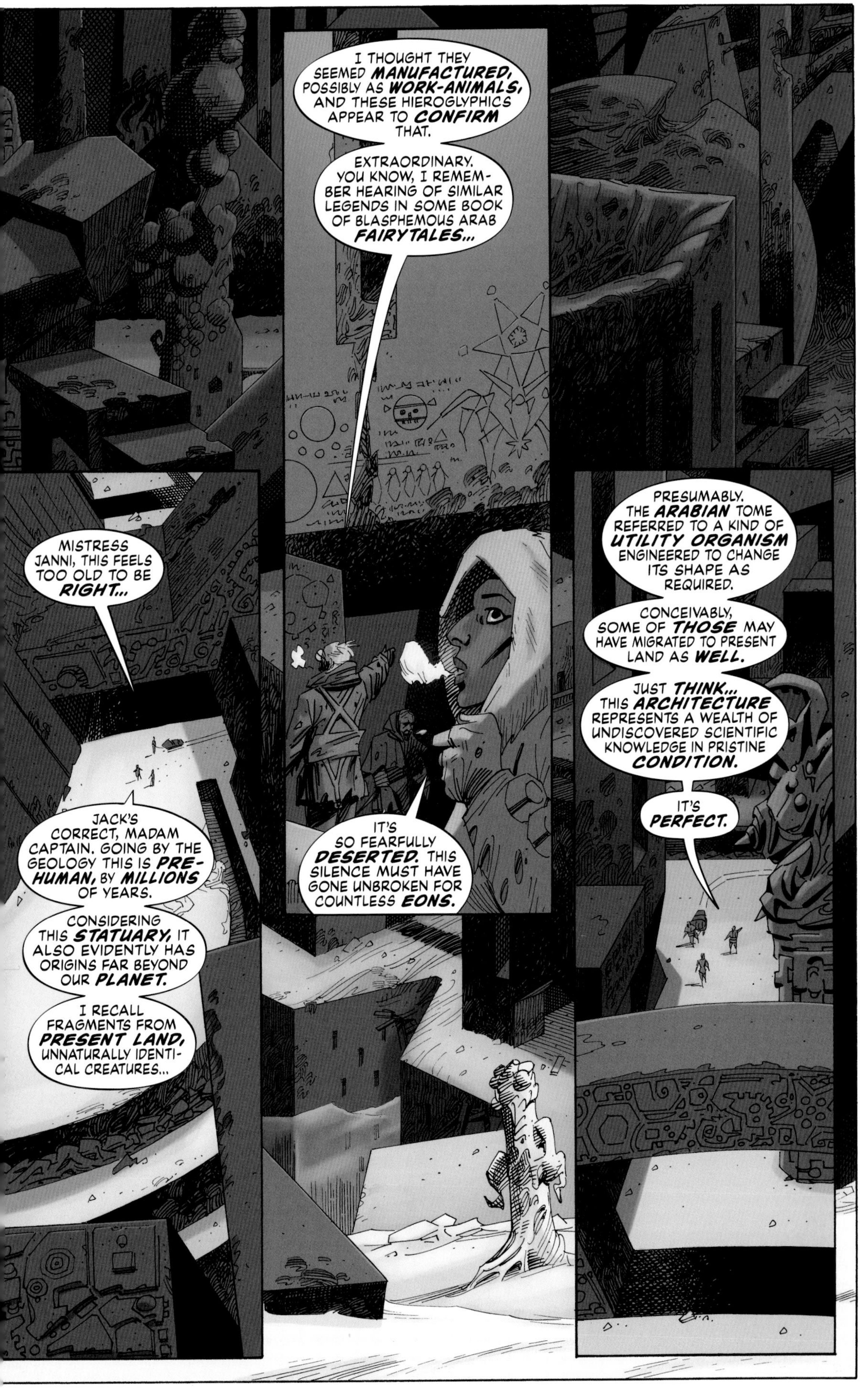
MISTRESS JANNI, THIS FEELS TOO OLD TO BE RIGHT...
JACK'S CORRECT, MADAM CAPTAIN. GOING BY THE GEOLOGY THIS IS PRE-HUMAN, BY MILLIONS OF YEARS.
CONSIDERING THIS STATUARY, IT ALSO EVIDENTLY HAS ORIGINS FAR BEYOND OUR PLANET.
I RECALL FRAGMENTS FROM PRESENT LAND, UNNATURALLY IDENTICAL CREATURES...
I THOUGHT THEY SEEMED MANUFACTURED, POSSIBLY AS WORK-ANIMALS, AND THESE HIEROGLYPHICS APPEAR TO CONFIRM THAT.
EXTRAORDINARY. YOU KNOW, I REMEMBER HEARING OF SIMILAR LEGENDS IN SOME BOOK OF BLASPHEMOUS ARAB FAIRYTALES...
IT'S SO FEARFULLY DESERTED. THIS SILENCE MUST HAVE GONE UNBROKEN FOR COUNTLESS EONS.
PRESUMABLY. THE ARABIAN TOME REFERRED TO A KIND OF UTILITY ORGANISM ENGINEERED TO CHANGE ITS SHAPE AS REQUIRED.
CONCEIVABLY, SOME OF THOSE MAY HAVE MIGRATED TO PRESENT LAND AS WELL.
JUST THINK... THIS ARCHITECTURE REPRESENTS A WEALTH OF UNDISCOVERED SCIENTIFIC KNOWLEDGE IN PRISTINE CONDITION.
IT'S PERFECT.

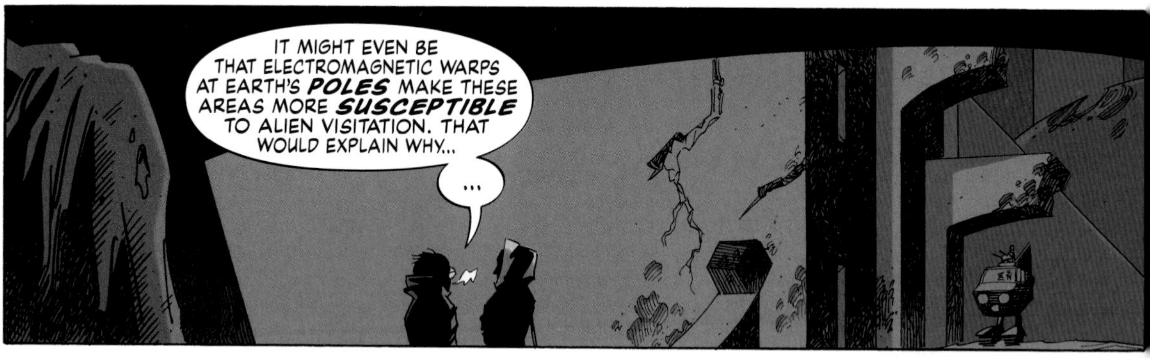
IT MIGHT EVEN BE THAT ELECTROMAGNETIC WARPS AT EARTH'S POLES MAKE THESE AREAS MORE SUSCEPTIBLE TO ALIEN VISITATION. THAT WOULD EXPLAIN WHY...
...

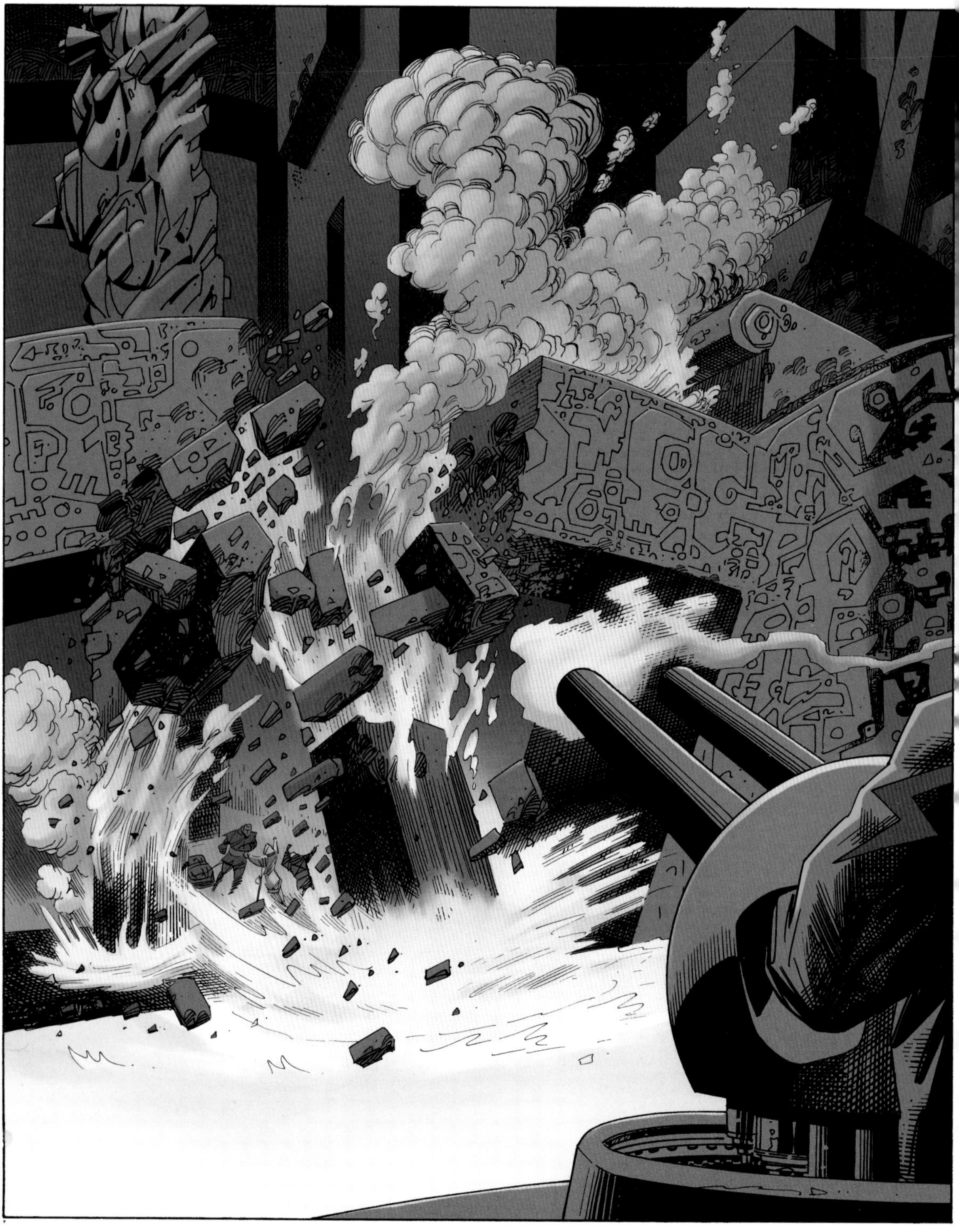

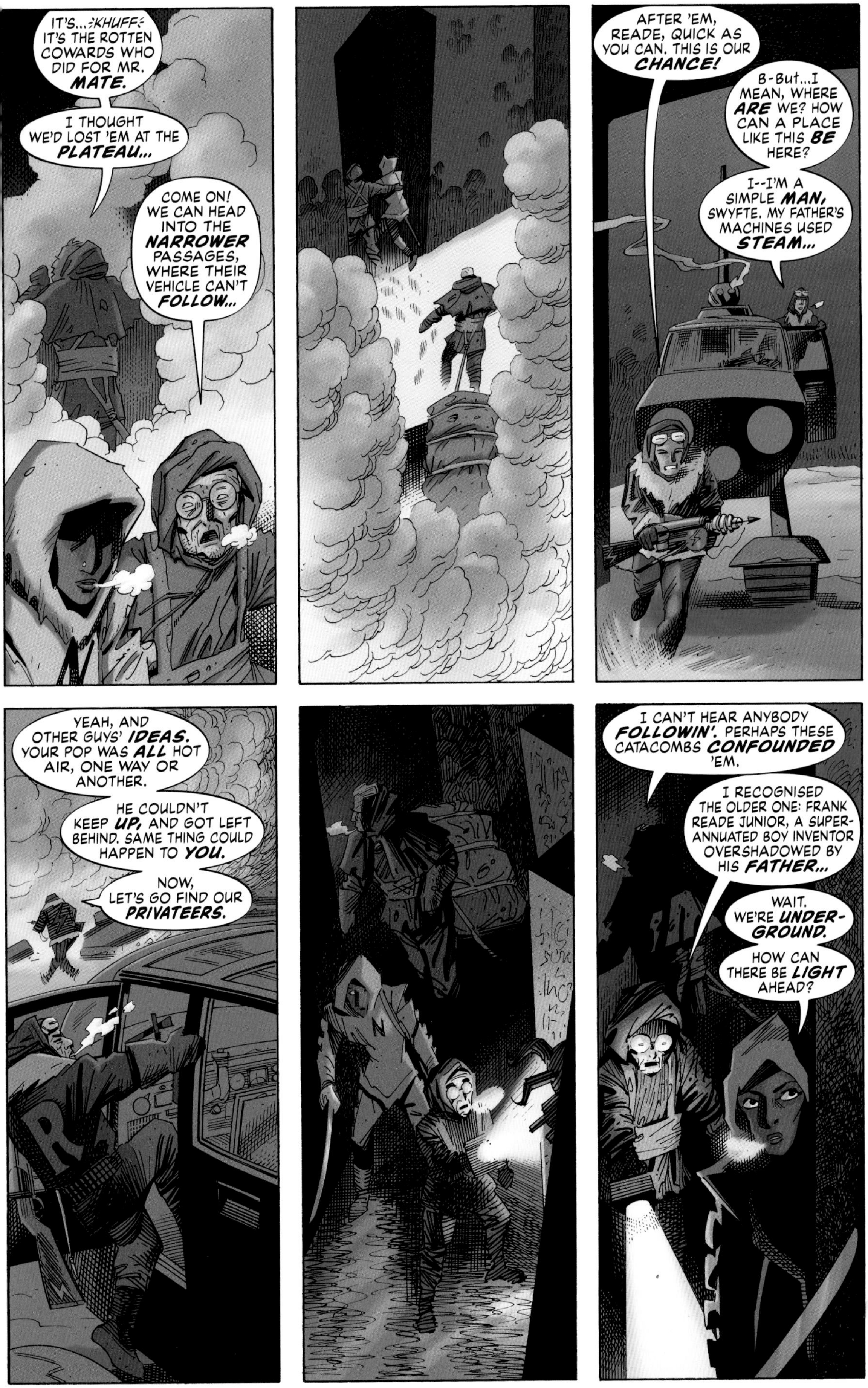
IT'S...KHUFF... IT'S THE ROTTEN COWARDS WHO DID FOR MR. MATE.
I THOUGHT WE'D LOST 'EM AT THE PLATEAU...
COME ON! WE CAN HEAD INTO THE NARROWER PASSAGES, WHERE THEIR VEHICLE CAN'T FOLLOW...
AFTER 'EM, READE, QUICK AS YOU CAN. THIS IS OUR CHANCE!
B-But...I MEAN, WHERE ARE WE? HOW CAN A PLACE LIKE THIS BE HERE?
I--I'M A SIMPLE MAN, SWYFTE. MY FATHER'S MACHINES USED STEAM...
YEAH, AND OTHER GUYS' IDEAS. YOUR POP WAS ALL HOT AIR, ONE WAY OR ANOTHER.
HE COULDN'T KEEP UP, AND GOT LEFT BEHIND. SAME THING COULD HAPPEN TO YOU.
NOW, LET'S GO FIND OUR PRIVATEERS.
I CAN'T HEAR ANYBODY FOLLOWIN'. PERHAPS THESE CATACOMBS CONFOUNDED 'EM.
I RECOGNISED THE OLDER ONE: FRANK READE JUNIOR, A SUPER-ANNUATED BOY INVENTOR OVERSHADOWED BY HIS FATHER...
WAIT. WE'RE UNDER-GROUND.
HOW CAN THERE BE LIGHT AHEAD?

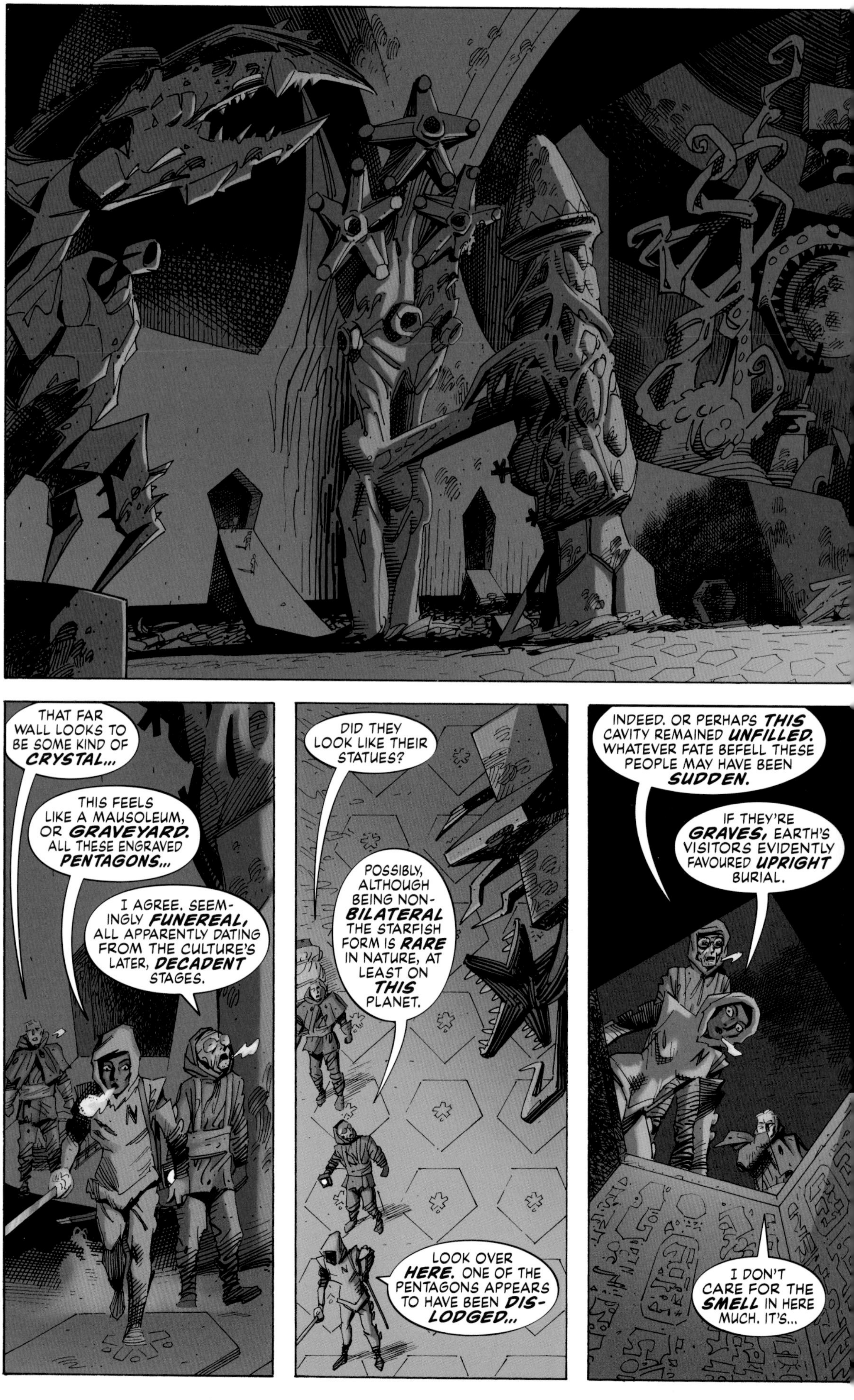
THAT FAR WALL LOOKS TO BE SOME KIND OF CRYSTAL...
THIS FEELS LIKE A MAUSOLEUM, OR GRAVEYARD. ALL THESE ENGRAVED PENTAGONS...
I AGREE. SEEM-INGLY FUNEREAL, ALL APPARENTLY DATING FROM THE CULTURE'S LATER, DECADENT STAGES.
DID THEY LOOK LIKE THEIR STATUES?
POSSIBLY, ALTHOUGH BEING NON-BILATERAL THE STARFISH FORM IS RARE IN NATURE, AT LEAST ON THIS PLANET.
LOOK OVER HERE. ONE OF THE PENTAGONS APPEARS TO HAVE BEEN DIS-LODGED...
INDEED. OR PERHAPS THIS CAVITY REMAINED UNFILLED. WHATEVER FATE BEFELL THESE PEOPLE MAY HAVE BEEN SUDDEN.
IF THEY'RE GRAVES, EARTH'S VISITORS EVIDENTLY FAVOURED UPRIGHT BURIAL.
I DON'T CARE FOR THE SMELL IN HERE MUCH. IT'S...

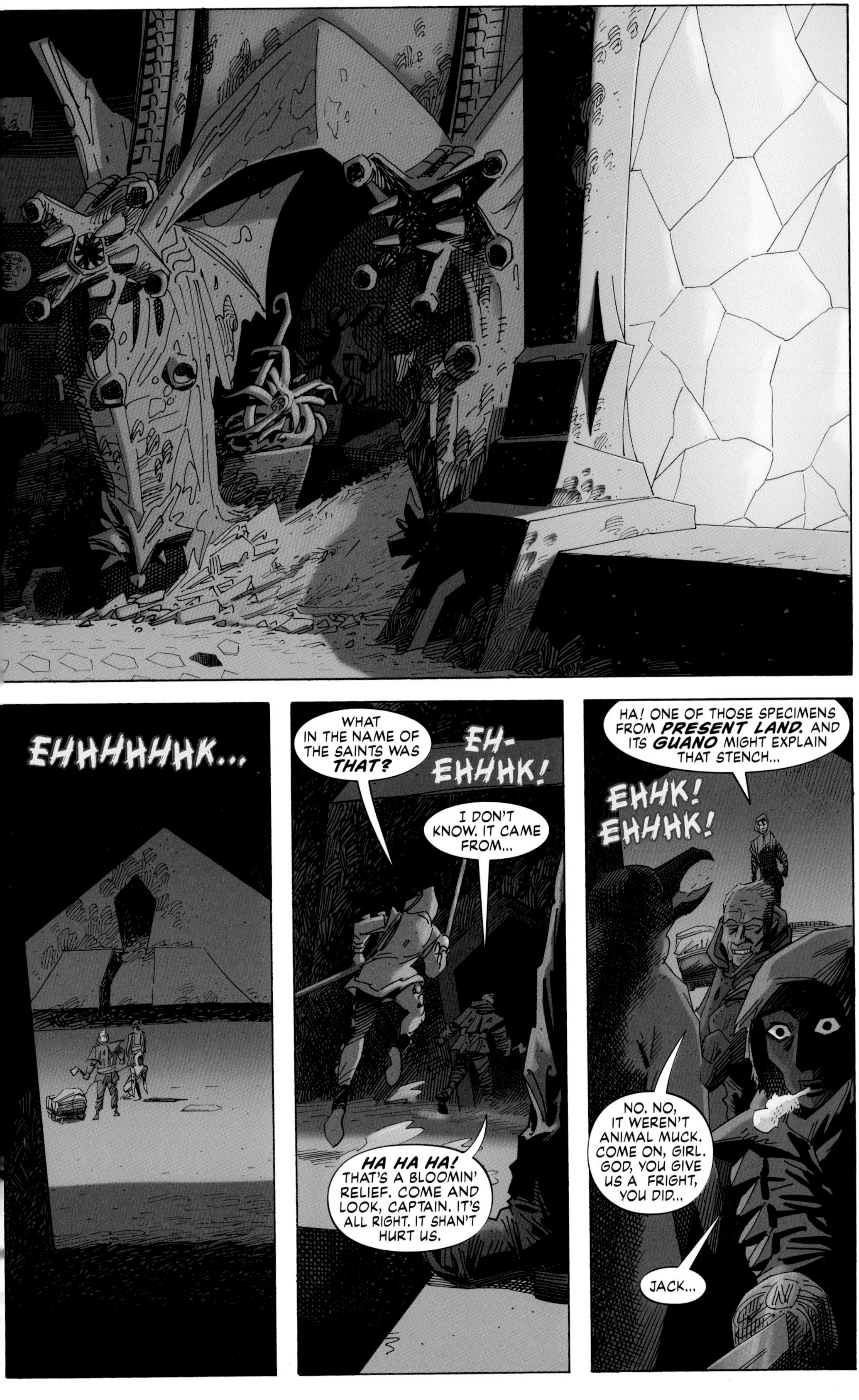
EHHHHHHK...
WHAT IN THE NAME OF THE SAINTS WAS THAT?
EH-EHHHK!
I DON'T KNOW. IT CAME FROM...
HA HA HA! THAT'S A BLOOMIN' RELIEF. COME AND LOOK, CAPTAIN. IT'S ALL RIGHT. IT SHAN'T HURT US.
HA! ONE OF THOSE SPECIMENS FROM PRESENT LAND. AND ITS GUANO MIGHT EXPLAIN THAT STENCH...
EHHK! EHHHK!
NO. NO, IT WEREN'T ANIMAL MUCK. COME ON, GIRL. GOD, YOU GIVE US A FRIGHT, YOU DID...
JACK...

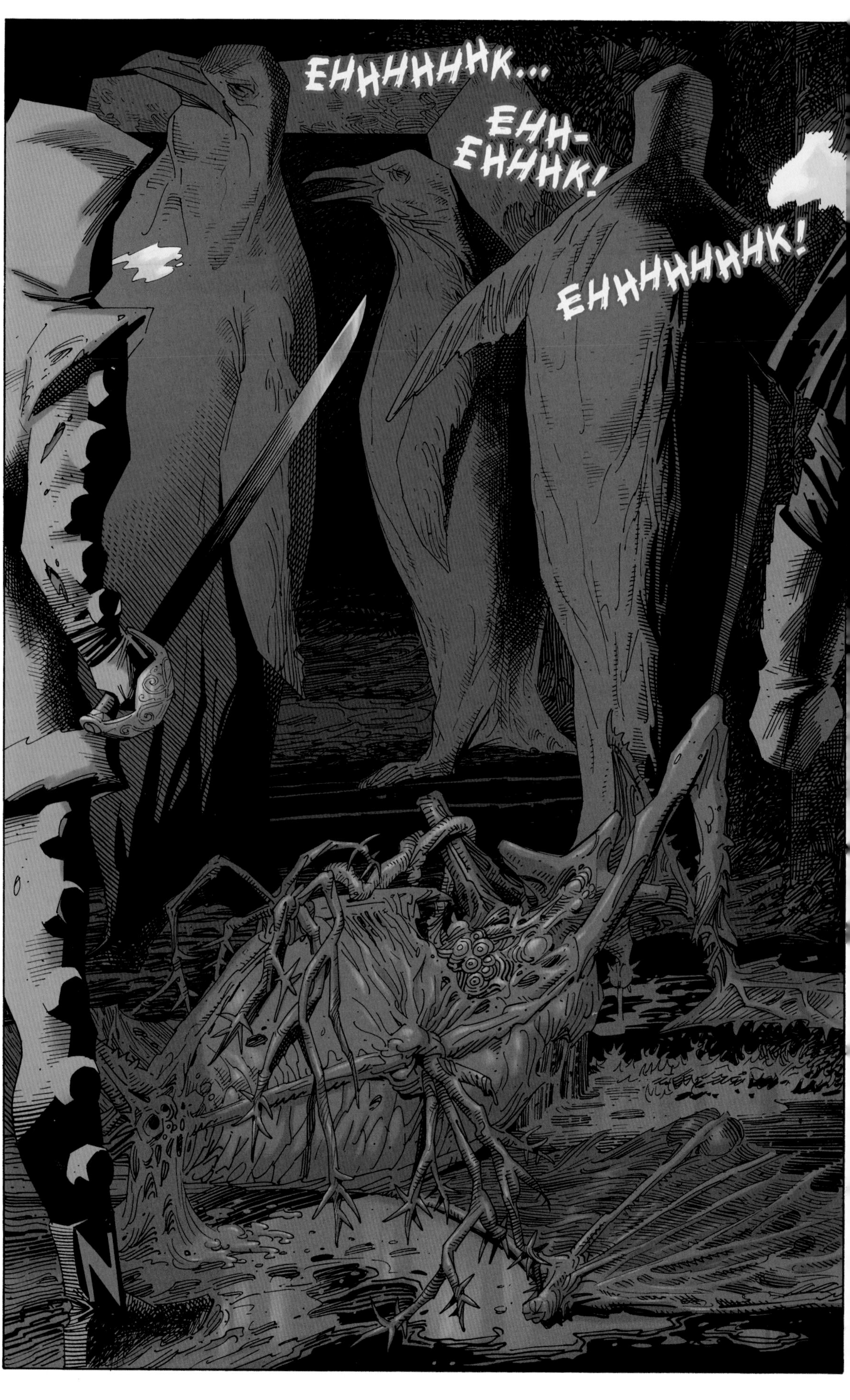
EHHHHHHK...
EHH-
EHHHK!
EHHHHHHHHK!

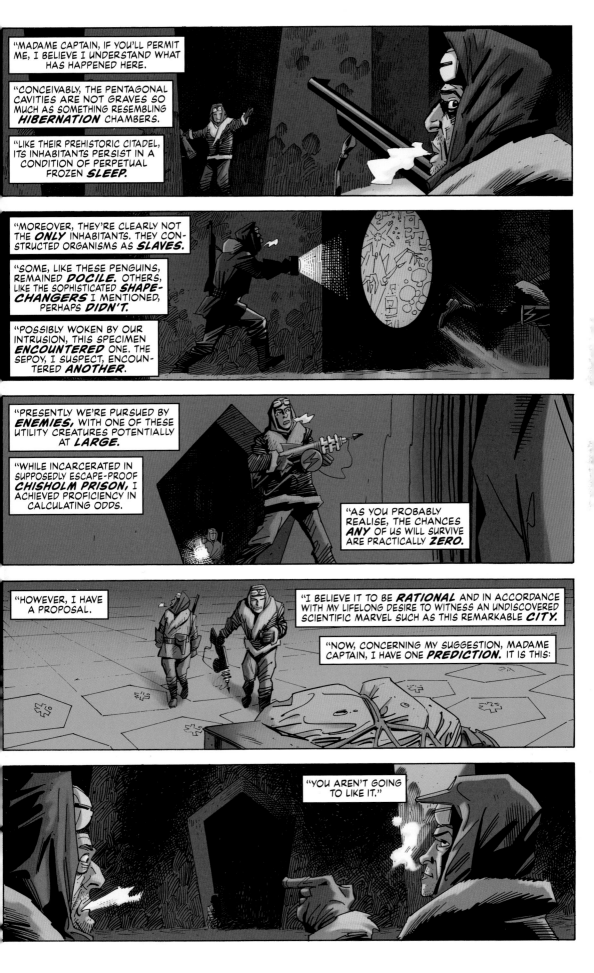

"MADAME CAPTAIN, IF YOU'LL PERMIT ME, I BELIEVE I UNDERSTAND WHAT HAS HAPPENED HERE.

"CONCEIVABLY, THE PENTAGONAL CAVITIES ARE NOT GRAVES SO MUCH AS SOMETHING RESEMBLING *HIBERNATION* CHAMBERS.

"LIKE THEIR PREHISTORIC CITADEL, ITS INHABITANTS PERSIST IN A CONDITION OF PERPETUAL FROZEN *SLEEP.*

"MOREOVER, THEY'RE CLEARLY NOT THE *ONLY* INHABITANTS. THEY CONSTRUCTED ORGANISMS AS *SLAVES.*

"SOME, LIKE THESE PENGUINS, REMAINED *DOCILE.* OTHERS, LIKE THE SOPHISTICATED *SHAPE-CHANGERS* I MENTIONED, PERHAPS *DIDN'T.*

"POSSIBLY WOKEN BY OUR INTRUSION, THIS SPECIMEN *ENCOUNTERED* ONE. THE SEPOY, I SUSPECT, ENCOUNTERED *ANOTHER.*

"PRESENTLY WE'RE PURSUED BY *ENEMIES,* WITH ONE OF THESE UTILITY CREATURES POTENTIALLY AT *LARGE.*

"WHILE INCARCERATED IN SUPPOSEDLY ESCAPE-PROOF *CHISHOLM PRISON,* I ACHIEVED PROFICIENCY IN CALCULATING ODDS.

"AS YOU PROBABLY REALISE, THE CHANCES *ANY* OF US WILL SURVIVE ARE PRACTICALLY *ZERO.*

"HOWEVER, I HAVE A PROPOSAL.

"I BELIEVE IT TO BE *RATIONAL* AND IN ACCORDANCE WITH MY LIFELONG DESIRE TO WITNESS AN UNDISCOVERED SCIENTIFIC MARVEL SUCH AS THIS REMARKABLE *CITY.*

"NOW, CONCERNING MY SUGGESTION, MADAME CAPTAIN, I HAVE ONE *PREDICTION.* IT IS THIS:

"YOU AREN'T GOING TO LIKE IT."

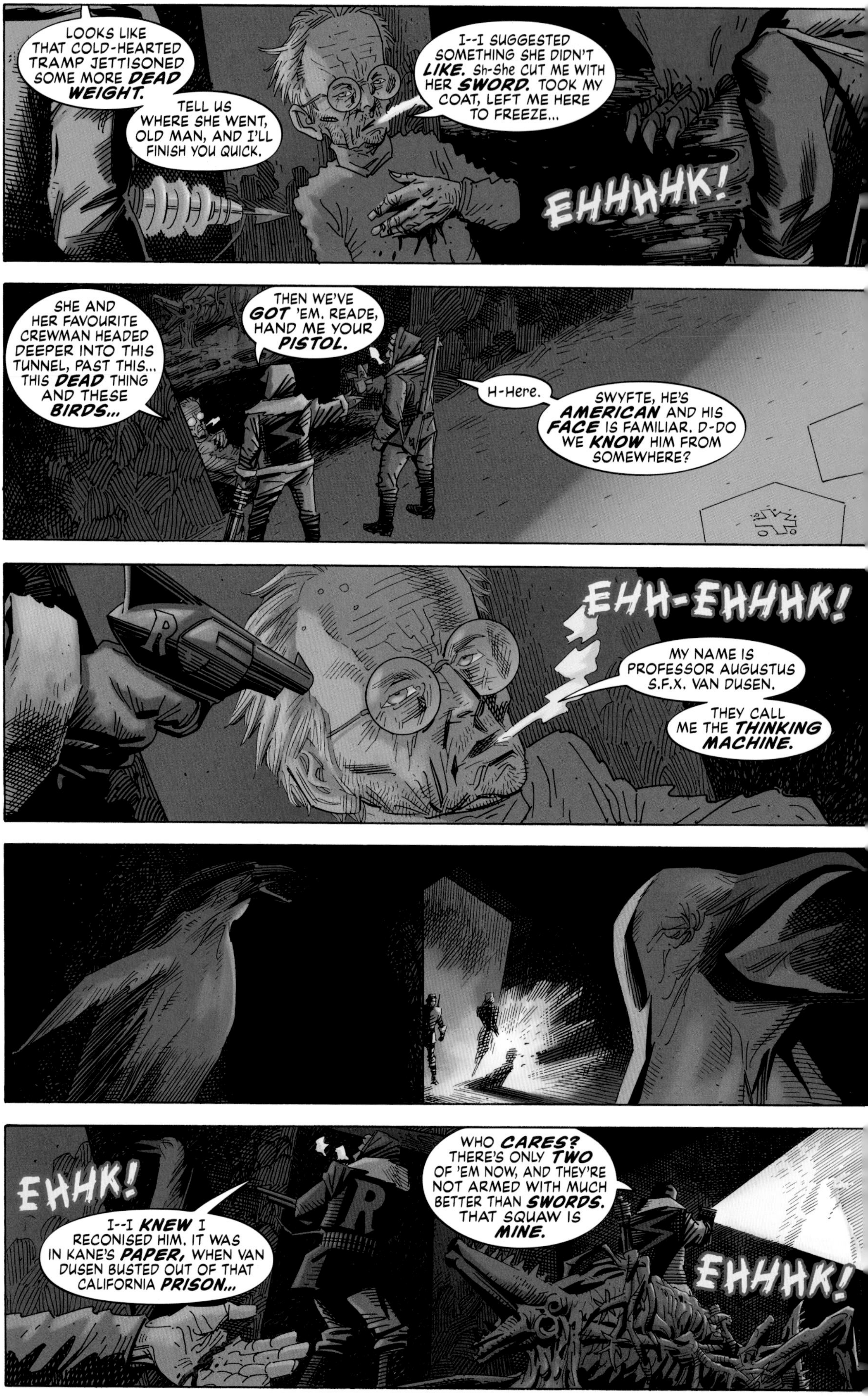
LOOKS LIKE THAT COLD-HEARTED TRAMP JETTISONED SOME MORE DEAD WEIGHT.
TELL US WHERE SHE WENT, OLD MAN, AND I'LL FINISH YOU QUICK.
I--I SUGGESTED SOMETHING SHE DIDN'T LIKE. Sh-She CUT ME WITH HER SWORD. TOOK MY COAT, LEFT ME HERE TO FREEZE...
EHHHHK!
SHE AND HER FAVOURITE CREWMAN HEADED DEEPER INTO THIS TUNNEL, PAST THIS... THIS DEAD THING AND THESE BIRDS...
THEN WE'VE GOT 'EM. READE, HAND ME YOUR PISTOL.
H-Here.
SWYFTE, HE'S AMERICAN AND HIS FACE IS FAMILIAR. D-DO WE KNOW HIM FROM SOMEWHERE?
EHH-EHHHK!
MY NAME IS PROFESSOR AUGUSTUS S.F.X. VAN DUSEN.
THEY CALL ME THE THINKING MACHINE.
EHHK!
I--I KNEW I RECONISED HIM. IT WAS IN KANE'S PAPER, WHEN VAN DUSEN BUSTED OUT OF THAT CALIFORNIA PRISON...
WHO CARES? THERE'S ONLY TWO OF 'EM NOW, AND THEY'RE NOT ARMED WITH MUCH BETTER THAN SWORDS. THAT SQUAW IS MINE.
EHHHK!

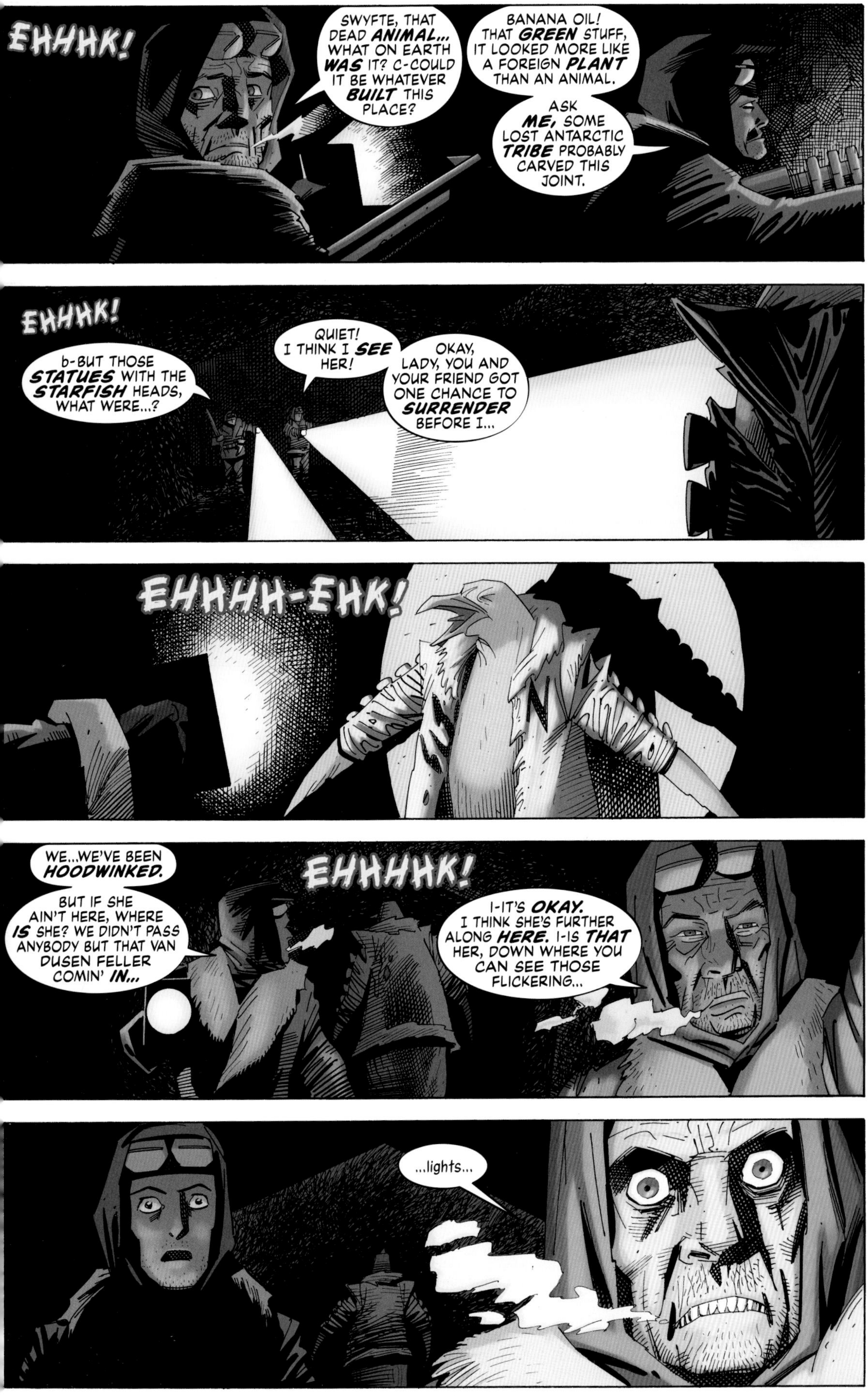
EHHHK!
SWYFTE, THAT DEAD ANIMAL... WHAT ON EARTH WAS IT? C-COULD IT BE WHATEVER BUILT THIS PLACE?
BANANA OIL! THAT GREEN STUFF, IT LOOKED MORE LIKE A FOREIGN PLANT THAN AN ANIMAL.
ASK ME, SOME LOST ANTARCTIC TRIBE PROBABLY CARVED THIS JOINT.
EHHHK!
b-BUT THOSE STATUES WITH THE STARFISH HEADS, WHAT WERE...?
QUIET! I THINK I SEE HER!
OKAY, LADY, YOU AND YOUR FRIEND GOT ONE CHANCE TO SURRENDER BEFORE I...
EHHHH-EHK!
WE...WE'VE BEEN HOODWINKED.
BUT IF SHE AIN'T HERE, WHERE IS SHE? WE DIDN'T PASS ANYBODY BUT THAT VAN DUSEN FELLER COMIN' IN...
EHHHHK!
I-IT'S OKAY. I THINK SHE'S FURTHER ALONG HERE. I-IS THAT HER, DOWN WHERE YOU CAN SEE THOSE FLICKERING...
...lights...

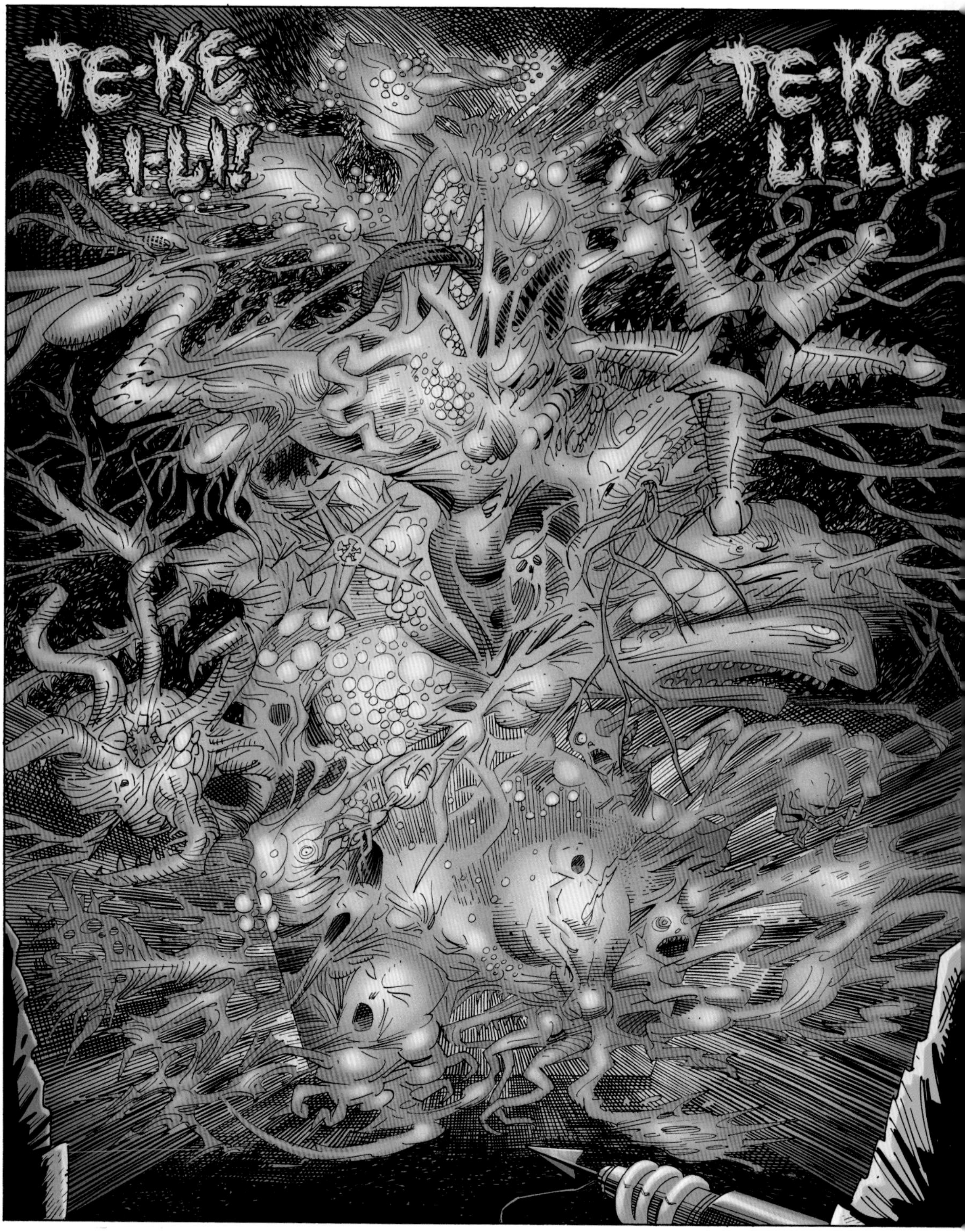
TE-KE-LI-LI!!
TE-KE-LI-LI!!

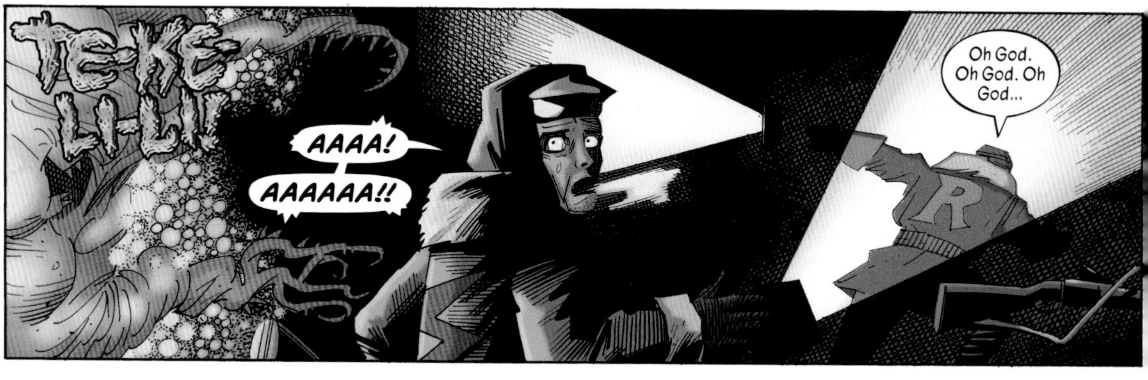
TE-KE-LI-LI!!
AAAA!
AAAAAA!!
Oh God. Oh God. Oh God...

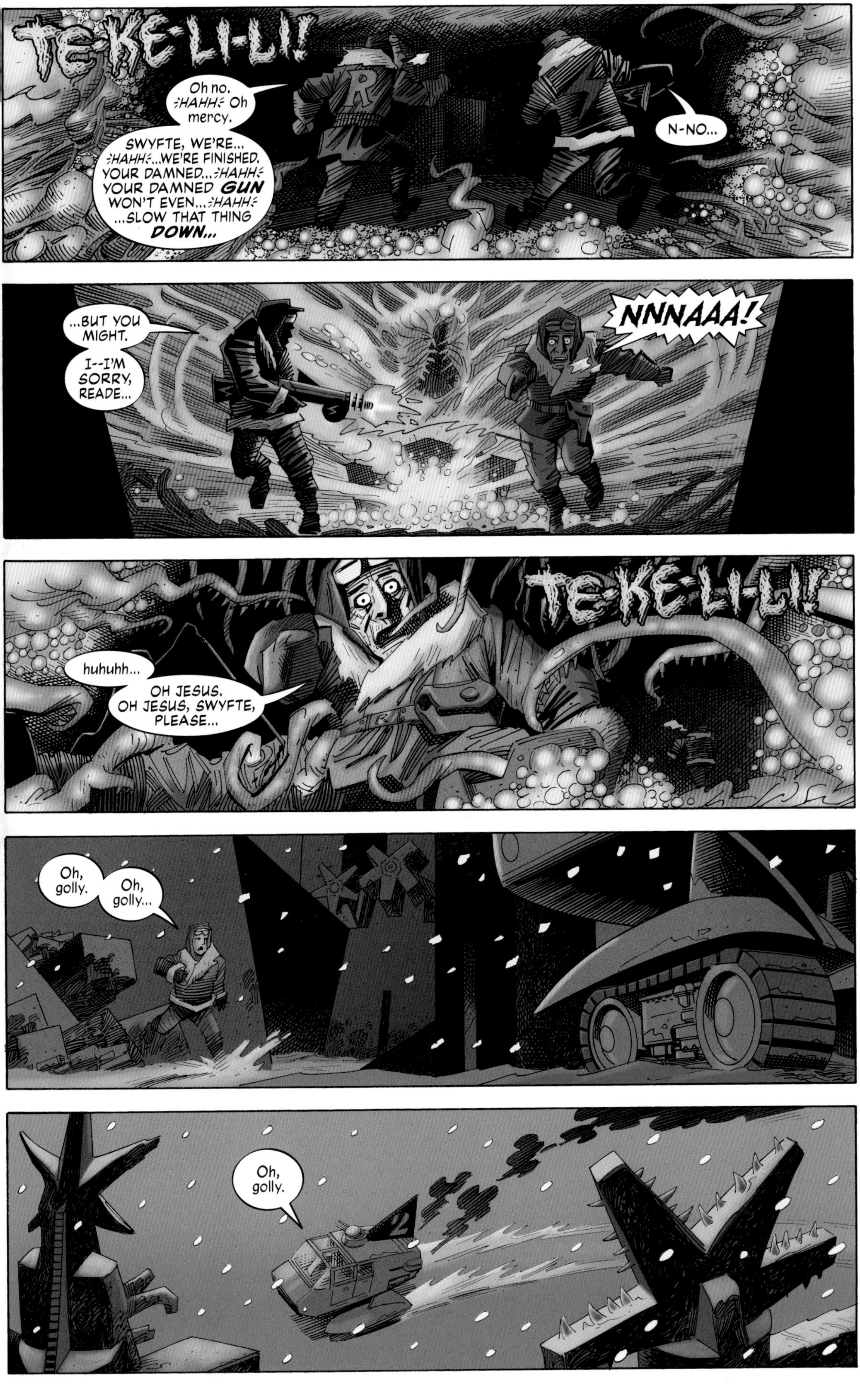

TE-KE-LI-LI!
Oh no. HAHH Oh mercy.
SWYFTE, WE'RE... HAHH ...WE'RE FINISHED. YOUR DAMNED... HAHH YOUR DAMNED GUN WON'T EVEN... HAHH ...SLOW THAT THING DOWN...
N-NO...
...BUT YOU MIGHT.
I--I'M SORRY, READE...
NNNAAA!
TE-KE-LI-LI!
huhuhh...
OH JESUS. OH JESUS, SWYFTE, PLEASE...
Oh, golly.
Oh, golly...
Oh, golly.

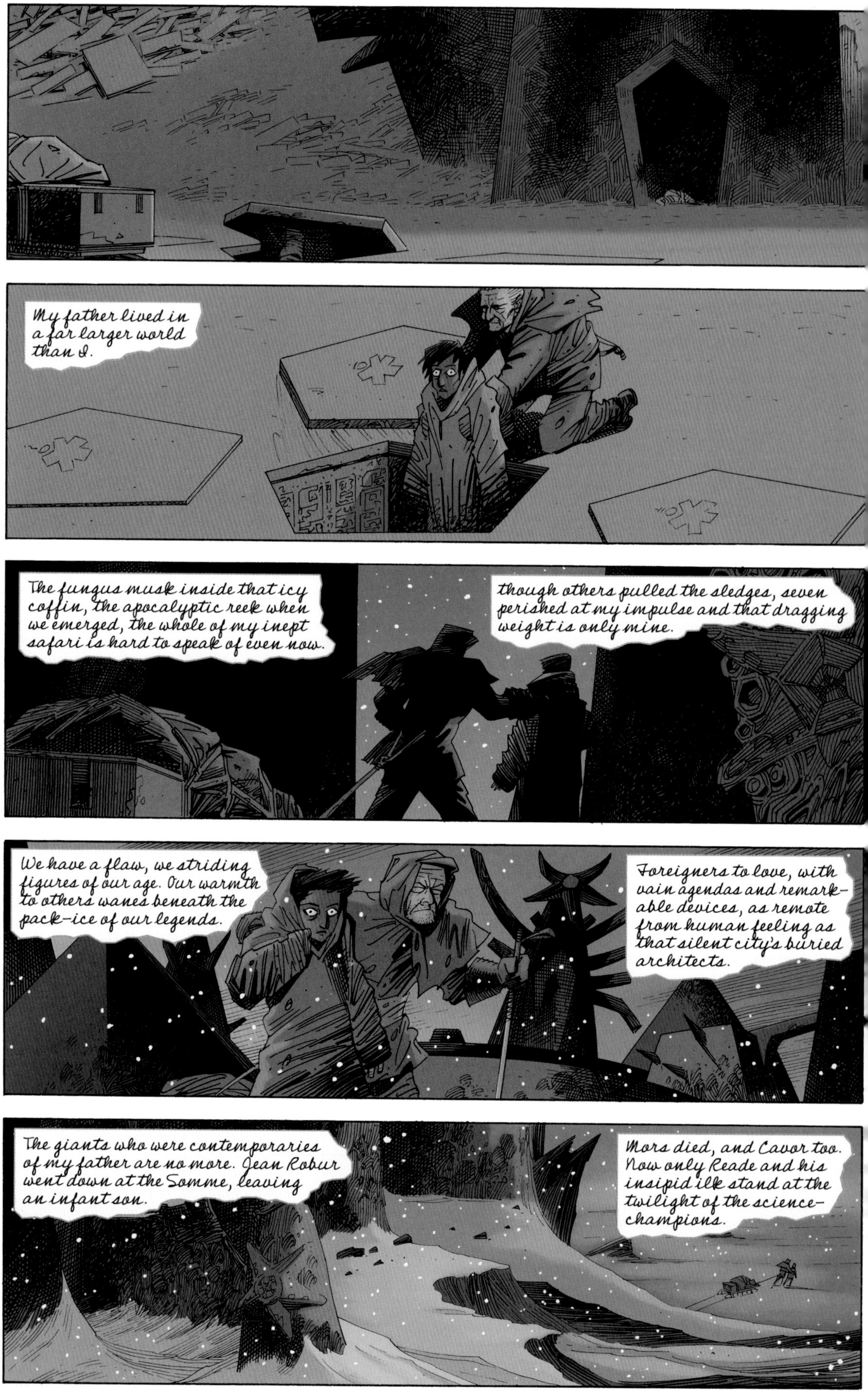
My father lived in a far larger world than I.
The fungus musk inside that icy coffin, the apocalyptic reek when we emerged, the whole of my inept safari is hard to speak of even now.
though others pulled the sledges, seven perished at my impulse and that dragging weight is only mine.
We have a flaw, we striding figures of our age. Our warmth to others wanes beneath the pack-ice of our legends.
Foreigners to love, with vain agendas and remark-able devices, as remote from human feeling as that silent city's buried architects.
The giants who were contemporaries of my father are no more. Jean Robur went down at the Somme, leaving an infant son.
Mors died, and Cavor too. Now only Reade and his insipid ilk stand at the twilight of the science-champions.

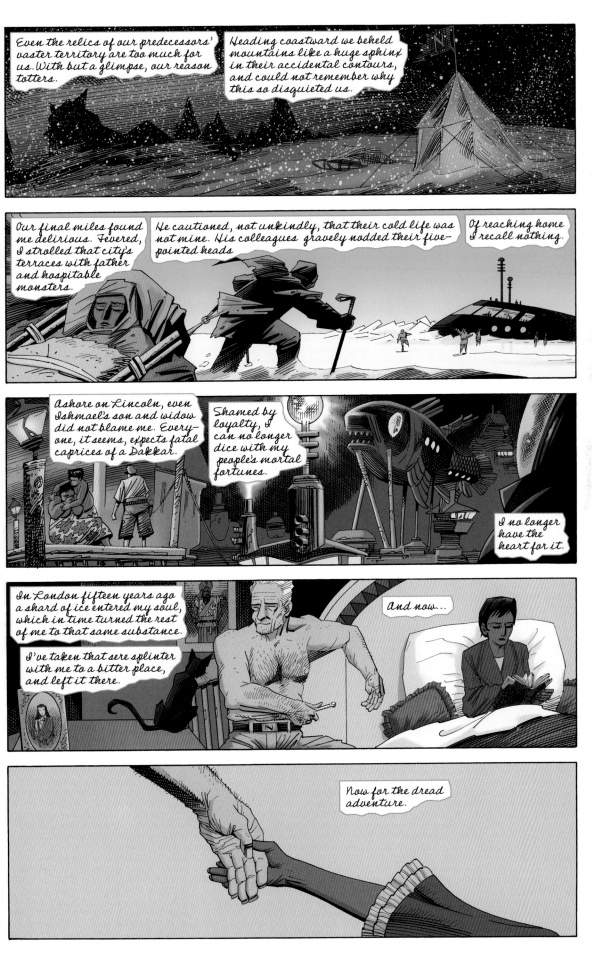

Even the relics of our predecessors' vaster territory are too much for us. With but a glimpse, our reason totters.

Heading coastward we beheld mountains like a huge sphinx in their accidental contours, and could not remember why this so disquieted us.

Our final miles found me delirious. Fevered, I strolled that city's terraces with father and hospitable monsters.

He cautioned, not unkindly, that their cold life was not mine. His colleagues gravely nodded their five-pointed heads

Of reaching home I recall nothing.

Ashore on Lincoln, even Ishmael's son and widow did not blame me. Everyone, it seems, expects fatal caprices of a Dakkar.

Shamed by loyalty, I can no longer dice with my people's mortal fortunes.

I no longer have the heart for it.

In London fifteen years ago a shard of ice entered my soul, which in time turned the rest of me to that same substance.

I've taken that sere splinter with me to a bitter place, and left it there.

And now...

Now for the dread adventure.

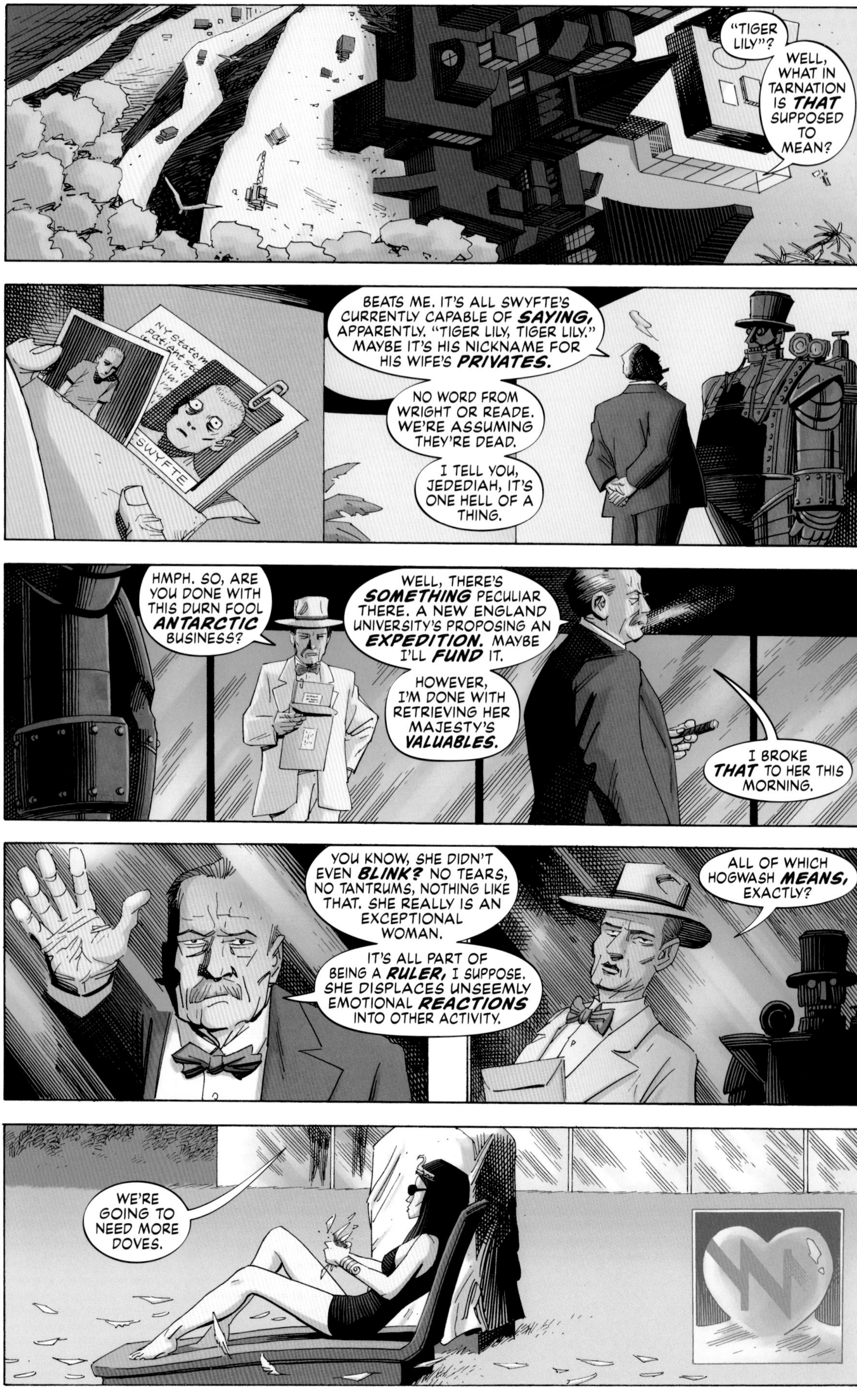
"TIGER LILY"?
WELL, WHAT IN TARNATION IS THAT SUPPOSED TO MEAN?
SWYFTE
BEATS ME. IT'S ALL SWYFTE'S CURRENTLY CAPABLE OF SAYING, APPARENTLY. "TIGER LILY, TIGER LILY." MAYBE IT'S HIS NICKNAME FOR HIS WIFE'S PRIVATES.
NO WORD FROM WRIGHT OR READE. WE'RE ASSUMING THEY'RE DEAD.
I TELL YOU, JEDEDIAH, IT'S ONE HELL OF A THING.
HMPH. SO, ARE YOU DONE WITH THIS DURN FOOL ANTARCTIC BUSINESS?
WELL, THERE'S SOMETHING PECULIAR THERE. A NEW ENGLAND UNIVERSITY'S PROPOSING AN EXPEDITION. MAYBE I'LL FUND IT.
HOWEVER, I'M DONE WITH RETRIEVING HER MAJESTY'S VALUABLES.
I BROKE THAT TO HER THIS MORNING.
YOU KNOW, SHE DIDN'T EVEN BLINK? NO TEARS, NO TANTRUMS, NOTHING LIKE THAT. SHE REALLY IS AN EXCEPTIONAL WOMAN.
IT'S ALL PART OF BEING A RULER, I SUPPOSE. SHE DISPLACES UNSEEMLY EMOTIONAL REACTIONS INTO OTHER ACTIVITY.
ALL OF WHICH HOGWASH MEANS, EXACTLY?
WE'RE GOING TO NEED MORE DOVES.

# A PERFECT MATCH...
# AND A PERFECT FUSE!
## ≡ by Staff Writer Hildy Johnson ≡

AS REGULAR READERS will surely be aware, my own view of wedlock is that everything in a marriage is incredibly hard except when, ideally, you'd like it to be. This notwithstanding, it was with some minor qualms and major highballs that your humble correspondent found herself in the receipt of an exclusive invitation to what might well be the big event of 1938, assuming that Frau Hynkel's little boy will be content to just sit fidgeting there in the Reichstag for a short while longer.

The affair in question, an impending matrimonial extravaganza between two of the world's most enduring piratical dynasties, to be conducted on a fogbound and uncharted island in the South Atlantic with a guest list of bloodthirsty criminals and without guarantee of coming back alive or unmolested, was of course completely irresistible. Being picked up from the Chicago waterfront at midnight (and let's face it, girls, who hasn't been?) only to be transported in a jet-black and deliriously baroque submersible crewed largely by unshaven murderesses for the next ten days was therefore something of a disappointment. Temporarily in charge of our unusual vessel, the infamous *Nautilus* of getting-on-a-century's maritime notoriety, the strapping Mistress Sally Kidd at least provided some relief from the monotony of our confinement with her easy access to the actual captain's potent and voluminous supplies of rum. Despite her being seemingly the latest in a line of ocean-hardened privateers, I can with some considerable smugness make report that I was able to drink Mistress Kidd beneath the table. Fortunately, shortly after that she proved entirely capable of eating me beneath the table so that we were even, and with more than honor satisfied.

Eventually, apparently somewhere within the mistenshrouded purlieus of the Riallaro Archipelago, we put to shore upon the well-established pirate sanctuary known as Lincoln Island. For those out there of insufficiently broad education, not to mention all the educated broads among my readership who may be insufficiently awake at this time of the afternoon, such wild freebooter havens were a feature of seafaring life back in the 17th and 18th centuries, anarchic and communitarian endeavours where society's excluded factions, be they criminal or theological, political or sexual, might congregate beyond the reach of legislation and polite society. Now, obviously, here in the U.S. with our plain-speaking ways we have our own word for a lawless and amoral enclave of this kind, and that word is "Chicago," but elsewhere, as I have pointed out before, they do things differently.

Nowhere more so, it seems, than Lincoln Island. First established in the middle 19th century by Sikh aristocrat turned science-buccaneer Prince Dakkar, known more generally as the first Captain Nemo, Lincoln Island is believed to be the last of these brigand utopias and, judging from appearances, was never really typical of timber-shivering renegade societies like those mentioned above. The same eye-popping engineering know-how that's apparent in the various successive versions of Prince Dakkar's much-feared submarine has obviously been applied to every structure on the island, with outlandishly designed and decorated chambers of unfathomable function raised on soaring metal stilts, while clustered at the bases of those mighty columns are the vivid and ingenious shanties of the lower ranks, including family homes and lean-to schools alongside teetering saloons and brothels. As I've previously indicated, all this was designed to make a gal feel properly at home.

You could say much the same for Lincoln Island's population, a flamboyant throng of lively ne'er-do-wells apparently collected from at least five quarters of the globe; a mix of perverts, pansies, crackpots, geniuses, poets, hopheads, prostitutes, thugs, communists, and howling babies that could only seem exotic to religious people living in the Catskills some two hundred years ago. In other words, the denizens of Lincoln are exactly like the people dwelling in those districts that you go to when you're after a good time. The only differences are that Lincoln's "district" is, by force of arms, a sovereign nation in its own right, and that rather than our much-loved "Chicago pianos" you're more likely to find Lincoln's residents practicing scales on belt-fed automatic harpoon-pistols.

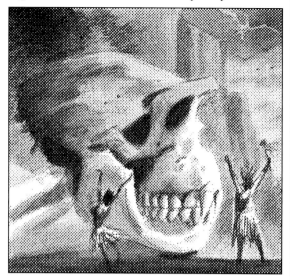

On arrival I was greeted by a stocky fellow in his later twenties of what seemed mixed Polynesian and Anglo-Saxon parentage, who introduced himself as one Tobias Ishmael and announced that I should be escorted to the elevated cabin occupied by Lincoln Island's ruler and my hostess for this royal occasion, Princess Janni Dakkar. As successor to the island's architect and the inheritor of his still-unsurpassed subsurface vehicle, the princess is decidedly her father's daughter. Greeting me in a lofty reception room embellished by the plunder of a dozen lands and several centuries was an attractive and accomplished woman hindered by the mannerisms of a movie villain.

Blinking only every hour or so and with an evidently well-rehearsed ability in her deployment of intimidating pauses during otherwise congenial conversation, Princess Dakkar is, at 43 years old, the second Captain Nemo and has already acquired a reputation for relentless carnage that is equal to or even in excess of that afforded her illustrious predecessor. Starting her career with an unscheduled demolition and attendant massacre on the East London docks in 1910, this colourful example of what might once tactfully have been termed "an adventuress" went on to sub-aquatic grave-robbing in 1912 with her audacious, not to mention heartless, plundering of what had until then been thought to be the irrecoverable wreckage of the sunken *Titan*. During the Great War, the princess at least showed an even-handed attitude in her torpedoing and looting of both sides' seagoing vessels in that conflict. After several post-war years marked by increasingly discriminating robbery and homicide, in 1925 this latest blossom from the Dakkar bloodline slaughtered various employees of Charles Foster Kane while seizing valuables belonging to Kane's houseguest, the high-flying and despicably young-looking Queen Ayesha from the central African domain of Kor, who must be in her sixth decade if she's a day! Seemingly not content with this larcenous coup, Prince Dakkar's darling daughter went on to lure the revered and elderly American inventors Frank Reade Jr. and Jack

Wright Jr. to as-yet-unexplained deaths in Antarctica before the year was out.

Since then, admittedly, it would appear that Princess Dakkar has restrained herself to only the occasional atrocity or incident of international proportions, as with the princess's positively whimsical abduction during 1933 of the colossal simian cadaver being kept refrigerated by the New York Port Authority in the wake of a highly publicized and ultimately fatal rampage earlier that same year. As it transpired, the second Captain Nemo's motive for this jaw-unhinging heist was a capricious urge to see the huge ape's bones returned to its Skull Island birthplace following requests made to her by that island's natives. Lest my gentle reader come to the erroneous conclusion that the princess has become perhaps less fierce in recent years, I should point out that she still keeps her father's weatherproofed and varnished skull as an adornment of the underwater dreadnaught he bequeathed to her. But then, it's well known that us dames are prone to getting sentimental.

Dressed in a well-tailored trouser-suit of emerald green with something of a boyish, military cut about the sweeping frockcoat, the princess would not look out of place at this year's fashion-house extravaganzas were she only to forgo that rather worrying cutlass. Over cups of mint tea with her highness, I observed with admiration the exquisite manners and polite regard for etiquette that I have often noticed in those with the power to have one killed. The silence following our introduction went on for a good ten minutes before your intrepid gal reporter realized belatedly that Princess Dakkar was expecting her to ask a question and would sit there patiently without a word until she did so.

I confess that my initial query, which amounted to a rather tremulous "why have you brought me here?" was not of the exacting journalistic standard which I've led you to expect of me, although the princess seemed to take it in her leather-booted stride. She told me, in her somehow too-precise and flawless English, that as she had made plain in her letter, the occasion was the marriage of her daughter Hira to a somewhat older aeronautic renegade, French science-desperado Armand Robur. Although I myself am patently far too young to remember, I'm reliably informed that the groom's late lamented father, one Jean Robur, garnered quite a reputation at the end of the last century with an astounding flying warship known, charmingly, as the *Terror*. The princess explained to me, with nothing but the teensiest hint of talking to an ill-bred imbecile, that the impending union of these two families with their respective domination of both air and water signalled an important merger in the world of global piracy which she was eager to announce by virtue of its psychological effects upon intended victims and piratical competitors.

When I repeated my enquiry in amended form to ask why I specifically had been selected to attend the matrimonial celebrations, Princess Dakkar smiled.

"Your writings are a great source of amusement for me. I especially enjoy the witty turn of phrase which you deploy upon occasion, as in your descripion of myself, some several years since, as a 'warlord debutante.' That really is a very funny thing to say."

Having forgotten that particular *bon mot* before agreeing to my rendezvous down on the waterfront, regular readers of this column will appreciate that the intimidating silence mentioned earlier which followed this remark worked wonders for my cardiac percussion. Finally I asked the princess if she would at least allow me to adjust my girdle prior to the beheading, at which to my very great relief she laughed with a surprising musicality, then somewhat spoiled the effect by adding a (probably) mischievous "Of course." Pressing ahead with my interrogation in the hope of by this means at least forestalling execution, I asked Princess Dakkar if I might be shown around her island and perhaps allowed to meet her family in order to present a rounded portrait when I came to write my article. After a few nerve-shredding moments of consideration, the princess at length agreed to my request on the condition that she would herself escort me in my tour of her domain, explaining that it would be of necessity a brief one if she was to be returned in time for the incipient nuptials early in the afternoon. Thus, with these rules established, we set out on our peregrination through the teeming pirate capital, where muscular and tattooed fellows hurried to attend our every whim wherever we should venture in a manner that I must confess I could get used to, given the unlikely opportunity.

Perambulating in among the towering pylon struts of her ramshackle but unnervingly efficient and well-managed fiefdom, I began to understand how Janni Dakkar could make this whole set-up work so smoothly, and at the same time I realized why, despite their many similarities, the pirate stronghold to be found on Lincoln Island is in all truth nothing like the pirate stronghold found here in Chicago. Here, and by extension throughout every city in the western world, we have a mass of individual and often criminal agendas working in aggressive opposition to each other and to the agendas of the status quo. With Lincoln Island, on the other hand, we have a mass of individual and almost wholly criminal agendas working in complete cooperation with each other in a culture where blackguards and privateers have actually become the status quo. Upon this isle of criminals, incredibly, there is no crime; at least according to the genial villains that I got the chance to speak to, who assured me that "the Captain" would deal even-handedly and fairly with disputes when they arose. Apparently betrayal, whether to a rival enterprise or the authorities, is Lincoln Island's only capital offense, and in the words of the princess herself, "it simply never happens."

Further in our exploration of the isle's improbable facilities I was permitted entrance to the hollow mountain or volcano where the terribly impressive *Nautilus* is penned, wherein I gasped and cooed appreciatively as if existence itself depended on it, which, for all that I know, it may well have. The next stop on our slightly rushed tour of inspection was the recently completed airfield in the island's northern reaches, seemingly constructed as a gesture of convenience and great civility extended to the Robur clan. It was at any rate in this location that I got to feast my eyes (between my parted fingers) on that family's truly stupefying flying fortress, the appropriately-titled *Terror*. The enormous bulk of this nefarious mechanism was alone enough to bring on an attack of vertigo. Although by all accounts it has been modified from Jean Robur's original design by his inventive son, imagining an object of that monstrous size suspended in thin air above civilization's spires put me in mind of Mr. R. Magritte's similar gravity-annihilating masses, after viewing which I often find myself in the immediate need of a sit-down, frequently clinging to my armchair or the carpet for dear life.

Returning to the island's busy epicenter from this more outlying center of activity, the second part of my request was granted in a series of brisk introductions to the princess's immediate and impending family. First among these, caught in the act of dressing for his role in the forthcoming ceremony, was the princess's consort of some thirteen years, an admirably well-preserved (he's at least a septuagenarian - it must be the sea air) and splendidly proportioned roughneck, introduced with a fond "This is Jack." If my reading doesn't fail me, this would be the escapee transported convict turned freebooting corsair, famous in the later 19th century under the handle of "Broad Arrow Jack," a soubriquet the origins of which were instantly apparent from the moment that we blundered unannounced into his dressing room. Stripped to the waist agreeably, an adjective I seldom employ in descriptions of men in their seventies, the sizeable and black arrow tattoo emblazoned on his naked back as token of his previous confinement was sufficient to preclude my asking him about his quaint dime-novel name. Although apparently engaged in fitting his considerable form into a tailor-made tuxedo, obviously a mode of dress he had not previously encountered, he gave the impression of a thoughtful and entirely honest man with an almost inordinate devotion to his wife, these being traits which I'm reliably informed are rarely found among the civilized and law-abiding husbands of my closest feminine associates. For her part, in her husband's company the princess showed a genuinely sweet warmth and affection which could easily make one forget, if only for a moment, the spectacular amount of mayhem for which these two turtle-doves share the responsibility.

Quite different from the likeable and unpretentious Jack was the next stop on my itinerary, clipped and formal groom in waiting Armand Robur. Only four years old when his beloved father took the *Terror's* predecessor down in flames over the Somme during 1915, the younger Robur would seem, understandably perhaps, to have grown up into a rather sombre and resentful sort of aerobatic larcenist. Black-haired and with a carefully brushed beard to complement his bordering-on-the-preposterous elaborate dress uniform, the 27-year-old junior master of the world appeared impervious to your reporter's charms, addressing his abrupt reply to my sole question in disdainful French through the obliging medium of the pirate queen who'd shortly be his mom-in-law. I was informed, in no uncertain terms, that the boy Robur held America in low esteem for its reluctance when it came to taking sides in the expected conflict with Tomania and Germany and thus would not deign to engage in any further conversation with me, which was frankly a considerable relief.

Much more agreeable, albeit by some measure more disturbing, was my meeting with the young sky-mercenary's soon-to-be and even younger bride. Despite my previous announcement of the fact that Princess Dakkar and Broad Arrow Jack have been together as a couple for just thirteen years, my lack of any skills with math meant that I was unable to suppress a startled yelp when taken in to meet with Hira Dakkar, as she sat there being robed and intricately painted with red henna dye in preparation for the fast-approaching ceremonials. Hira Dakkar, a third-generation scourge of sea and sky, makes for a bride of near-heartbreaking beauty, although one who would seem to have just turned twelve. Call me old-fashioned, but even as one who has vacationed frequently below the Mason-Dixon line I found this state of affairs to be much too modern for my liking, though I'm led to understand that arranged marriages of this variety and sometimes at this tender age are an established feature of Hindu and Sikh traditions. As if sensing that there was a question which I was too ladylike to ask, once we were out of earshot of the baby bride-to-be, her mother made a great show of informing me that the arrangement in this case was nothing but consensual and there of course would be no consummation of the marriage for at least five years, which by my reckoning would still add up to some sort of a felony where I was raised. Besides, the princess added, with the likelihood of aerial warfare playing as significant a part as naval battles in the forthcoming expected conflagration, an alliance with the Roburs had become a tactical priority. Ain't young love grand?

Keen as I might be to impress you with my cosmopolitan and easy grasp of foreign cultures, I will readily confess that the protracted wedding service when it finally arrived was utterly unfathomable to me. It appeared to be a grossly over-hyphenated ceremony of innumerable installments, during which a staggering array of brightly-colored Indian confectionary was provided at what would appear to have been strictly-observed ritual intervals. At some point, luckily, the formal service of the afternoon gave way to a more customary alcohol-fueled celebration in the evening, after the exhausted bride had been provided with a decorous and seemly goodnight peck upon the cheek from her glum-looking hubby and then no doubt taken by her mother off to the familiar and toy-littered room that was to be her solitary bridal chamber. It was at this juncture that your fearless correspondent finally threw off her inhibitions and relaxed enough to enter into the inebriated spirit of this jubilant event. I'm told that I caused a sensation with my dancing, partnered by an entranced string of would-be world-enslaving megalomaniacs, some of whom were apparently quite taken with me if the mash-note I discovered in my stocking the next day from one "Count Zero" is an indication. This, admittedly, was upon waking with a frightful headache in my cabin on the *Nautilus* only to be informed by the redoubtable young Mistress Kidd

that I had slept or rather been unconscious for the previous eighteen hours and that we were already a good part of the way home, if not yet close enough to smell the pizza and the graft.

Cute as the couple were, her with the little ribbons in her hair and him with his distinguished epaulettes and hundred-ton airborne destroyer waiting on the island's lately-added airstrip, I must confess serious doubts regarding how long it can last, by which I am referring to the world and not to the relationship of these two newlyweds. Despite the awkward gap in age and culture they are both the children of implacable and very capable enemies of humanity, and I'm quite certain they'll be fine, it rather being all the rest of us that I'm concerned about. From where this gal is standing, the surely forthcoming war in Europe offers a bonanza for the Dakkar family business, and with even the serene blue heavens now in danger of attack one strains to think of anywhere that can be deemed entirely safe, except possibly sunny Lincoln Island.

Let's just hope the happy couple aren't planning on having offspring any time real soon. Some family trees, after all, have dangerous and unexpected critters hiding in them, *n'est ce pas?*

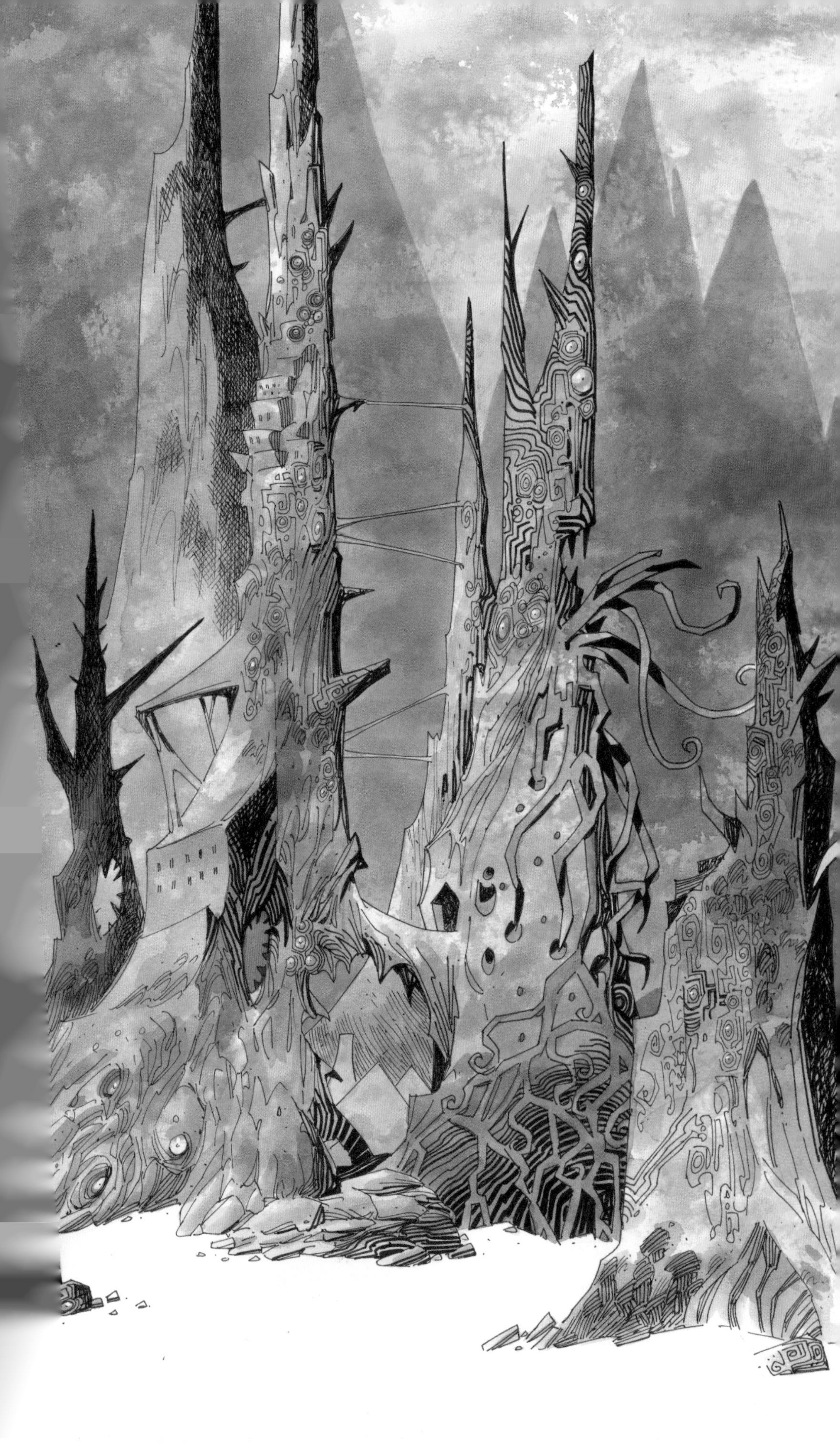